D0403440

THE LATE STARTERS
ORCHESTRA

THE LATE STARTERS ORCHESTRA

ARI L. GOLDMAN

ALGONQUIN BOOKS OF CHAPEL HILL   2014

Published by
Algonquin Books of Chapel Hill
Post Office Box 2225
Chapel Hill, North Carolina 27515-2225

a division of
Workman Publishing
225 Varick Street
New York, New York 10014

Portions of part 3 were previously published, in slightly
different form, in Ari L. Goldman, "Big Cello, Little Cello,"
New York Times, June 8, 2008.

Although this book depicts real events, some names have been changed to
protect the privacy of individuals, and some portions of the narrative timeline
have been condensed for simplicity.

Library of Congress Cataloging-in-Publication Data
Goldman, Ari L., [date]
The Late Starters Orchestra / Ari L. Goldman.
pages cm
ISBN 978-1-56512-992-4
1. New York Late Starters String Orchestra.   2. Orchestral musicians—
New York (State)—New York.   3. Cello—Instruction and study—New
York (State)—New York.   I. Title.
ML28.N5N37 2014
787.4092—dc23

[B]   2013044895

10 9 8 7 6 5 4 3 2 1
First Edition

To my brothers,
Shalom and Dov

"I have three messages.
One is we should never, ever give up.
Two is you never are too old to chase your dreams.
Three is it looks like a solitary sport, but it's a team."

—DIANA NYAD, 64, after completing
the 110-mile swim from from Cuba to Florida
on her fifth attempt.

CONTENTS

PART ONE: TUNING UP

The Fiddler   16

The Cello   31

PART TWO: OVERTURES

The Next Chapter   51

Origins   55

Love and Marriage   75

PART THREE:
FATHERS AND SONS AND ORCHESTRAS

Downtown Symphony   87

Milt   93

Suzuki   98

Music Moms and Dads   115

The InterSchool Orchestras of New York   123

Avery Fisher Hall   127

The Oldest Kid in the Orchestra   132

PART FOUR:
THE NEW YORK LATE-STARTERS
STRING ORCHESTRA

Conducting   159

Nishanti   164

Dan   167

Joe   173

LSO and Suzuki   179

The East London Late Starters Orchestra   184

The Really Terrible Orchestra   188

Shira   193

PART FIVE: OLD AND NEW

Bar Mitzvah   208

Practicing   214

The View from the Audience   217

Back in the Saddle   222

Music Camp British Style   225

Aaron   229

Geraldine   231

Ed, Colin, and Chris   233

The Maestros and Me   237

Music Camp American Style   245

PART SIX:
THE BEAUTY OF AN OPEN STRING

Happy Birthday   263

Finale   270

Grand Finale   277

Acknowledgments   289

THE LATE STARTERS

ORCHESTRA

PART ONE

TUNING UP

Boccherini

Vivaldi

Casals

Ma

Goldman

To be a musician is a curse. To *not* be one is even worse.
—Jazz trumpeter JACK DANEY

Standing in a crowded elevator in midtown Manhattan with a cello strapped to your back is no way to win a popularity contest. For one thing, you are taking up nearly twice your normal footprint; for another, you can barely make a move without sideswiping someone. But there I was jostling people with my cello in the elevator of a Manhattan loft building on my way to my very first rehearsal with the New York Late-Starters String Orchestra.

In truth, the cello on my back was the least of my worries. I was en route to what I feared would be a mortifying encounter. My orchestra experience was limited to playing in a middle-school ensemble with my son plus a handful of sessions with adult amateurs where I often felt lost and overwhelmed. Humiliation was assured. I was destined to play out of tune, out of time, out of rhythm—crimes akin to having your cell phone go off in a crowded theater. Why was I even going? I was silently praying that the elevator would get stuck on its slow climb to the thirteenth floor.

The elevator eventually belched me out into a narrow hallway that led to a small actors' studio where members of the orchestra were unpacking their instruments. The room was strewn with props from a show, including hats, shoes, and an old bed frame with exposed springs. There was a maze of pipes overhead and wire mesh–reinforced windows that were nailed shut. This old loft, which once housed a ladies coat factory, was surely on its way to becoming something else—luxury condominiums or maybe a swanky gym—but for this brief moment it was rehearsal space for the Late Starters Orchestra.

I had been advised to arrive ten minutes early because the Late Starters Orchestra was paying for the studio by the hour. And it wasn't about to start late. Casting a brief glance around, it became clear to me that the *late* in the orchestra's name referred to the age of the participants, not to the starting hour.

The players, a smattering in their thirties but most of them approaching sixty like me and still others well beyond it, were readying their instruments and setting up their music stands when the conductor—a tall, thin, blond, serious, and yet stunning-looking woman, decidedly younger than her late-starter participants—silenced us all with an A note from her violin. It's called "tuning," and we all did our best to get the A string on our instruments to match hers.

The A is the highest of the *four* strings on the cello. There are a thousand steps to making music in an ensemble but it all begins with making sure the instruments are in tune, which means, in effect, that everyone is on the same page.

Ari, mein liebe, I heard my late cello teacher, Mr. J, say gently. *I speak German. You speak Hebrew. But if you speak Hebrew and I speak German we cannot understand each other. We must find a common language and that common language for us is the key of E, English. You understand, right? In music, like in language, we must find common ground. When an orchestra tunes, that common ground is A.*

What's nice about the note A is that all the classical string instruments—the violin, the viola, the cello and the double bass—have an A as an open string. An *open string* means the note is played with just one hand, the right hand—the hand that holds the bow. No left hand pressure is necessary. There's a purity to this that enables a clear conversation to get going between all the instruments.

Here was something familiar to me. A, the highest

string on the cello, is my favorite letter, and not just because my name starts with A. I relate to A. For me it signals beginnings and taking chances—something I've tried to do both in my career as a journalist and in my religious life.

As the conductor played her A, I strained to listen to my cello's A. I could hear that it was off—my ear was that good—but I wasn't sure if I was too high or too low. I suddenly remembered a trick that Mr. J taught me. *The note is inside you,* he said. *Just sing it. Let it come out. Sing!* Even though everyone else was bowing, I was singing. I sang the A—"Aaaa," I sang above the din—until I could hear it and then try to match it on my cello. My A string, I now knew, was too low. I reached up to the top of the cello, turned the peg up a notch and suddenly—and remarkably—my A sounded exactly like all the others. It joined the great flow of A strings in the room, and through all time, and through all orchestras. It seemed like the most perfect sound I had ever heard. I experienced an inexpressible joy. I almost burst out laughing with the sheer delight of playing a single note. I remembered why I had come.

You are not playing a note. You are playing a song, Mr. J would say when I'd complain about having to play a note over and over and over again until it sounded the way he thought it should. *Every note is a song. Sing! Play it!*

Our A's in tune, the conductor raised her baton to be-gin. Suddenly, the door opened and a gray-haired woman in her seventies came rushing into the room with her cello. The conductor paused to allow the new cellist a chance to find a seat. For some reason, I felt an immediate connec-tion with this woman. Maybe it was because she reminded me of my Grandma Nettie, who will forever be associated in my mind with brownies so delicious we called them "yum yum cake." I waved at the woman to indicate that there was a place in the cello section next to me but then realized that there was no chair for her, just the old bed frame left over from the actors who normally used the room. I put down my cello and went into the hall in search of a folding chair for this grandma look-alike.

When I returned I positioned the chair between my-self and the bed frame. The woman took her seat, nodded her thanks, and then whispered, "Hi. I'm Eve. Now if they only got rid of the fucking bed, we'd have room to play."

Profanity was the last thing I expected to hear in this classical music environment. But that was before I met Eve and some of her brash and racy friends in their seventies. Although Eve looked like my grandmother, she didn't sound like her. But I was happy to have Eve next to me. She was a more experienced player and helped me find my way when I got lost in the score. My chief weakness as a player is rhythm, the vital necessity to keep a steady beat. But Eve was a metronome. Some musicians keep the beat in their heads; Eve was of the foot-tapping variety. With her next to me, I just followed her tapping foot. And, once again, she turned back into this maternal figure, keeping a steady pace. I was reminded of listening to my mother's heartbeat when I put my head on her breast as a young child. And it reminded me of another one of Mr. J's teachings: *Rhythm emerges from your body.*

Rhythm is the organizing principal of the natural world—and of our lives, too. Listen to your heartbeat. Listen to your breathing. Be aware of your footsteps. The beat is not something you have to learn. It is something you have to let come forth from your very being.

Including Eve and myself, there were eight cellists in our group that day as well as an equal complement of violinists plus two violists and one double bassist. To a classical music outsider, we were all playing the same string instrument made of wood, just ones in different sizes. In size, the violin is the smallest (at twenty-three inches, just slightly longer than the average newborn) and then up the scale to the viola (twenty-seven inches, a baby at nine months) to the cello (forty-eight inches, a preteen) to the double bass (sixty to seventy inches, a full-size adult). We were a family, unified by a similar look, but each with distinct hues and voices. At later rehearsals, we would be joined by additional string players, but we rarely numbered more than thirty instruments. Sometimes an amateur clarinetist or a flutist would wander into our rehearsal. We'd immediately spot them by the small instrument case they carried and we'd brace ourselves for the awkward conversation that would be sure to follow. "Sorry, but we're a string orchestra. Strings only." We'd direct them to other amateur ensembles that were full orchestras, such as the Downtown Symphony.

There's a lot you can do with a string orchestra. We played Dvořák, Offenbach, Vivaldi, and Mozart that first day alone. The music was challenging but possible. I avoided any major embarrassments.

As I settled in, I realized that Eve was among the most experienced players in the group, which was founded in 2007, two years before my first rehearsal with them. While I was looking to her for guidance, I saw others looking to me! Yes, I sometimes got lost on the page of music, but a woman named Margaret, even older than Eve, was having trouble finding the right page. I was to learn that Margaret was actually a competent musician who took the orchestra very seriously. Her main problem was that she was somewhat deaf and did not hear when the conductor announced what piece of music we were playing. She looked about anxiously to see what page we were on, but once the music started, she joined in. It seemed that her deafness was limited to speech; she could hear music quite well. This is something that many older players experience, perhaps because playing an instrument is not simply an aural sensation but a physical one as well. The musical vibrations can help you find your way. *The music comes from you and goes right back into you,* Mr. J said.

There are telltale signs of a cello beginner—colored tape on the neck of the cello (to indicate where to put the fingers of your left hand to get the right sound) and a red dot smack in the middle of the bow (to help you gage the distance you have left when playing a full bow). A middle-aged cellist named Mark had both. He called them his "crutches" and said that they got him through the session without making too many mistakes. He spent much of the first session playing what might be called "air cello," moving one's bow right over the string so that it looks like you are playing but not risking making a sound. "My ultimate crutch," he told me with a smile.

Clearly some of us did not know what we were doing,

but that didn't stop us. Built into the system was the reality that the more accomplished players (like Eve, and some even better) would carry the less adept, like Mark, and that, eventually, with repetition and hard work and support, everyone would be brought up to a higher musical level. Meeting Mark and others also helped me realize that my fears were unfounded. In this group of amateurs, I was more at the middle of the pack than at the bottom. I could play. I could contribute something to this orchestra.

Playing cello with this group made me part of something larger than myself. Although there was hardly any conversation between the players, a true sense of camaraderie developed. Without even talking, I could feel it in the air. As members of the New York Late-Starters String Orchestra, we were making music.

The founders of the orchestra insisted on using our full acronym—NYLSO—but I was tickled to use the shorter version, LSO. For classical music lovers, LSO means only one thing: the London Symphony Orchestra, one of the great music ensembles of the world. The idea that I had something in common with the LSO, if only three letters, was too delicious for me to pass up. I signed up as a cellist with NYLSO, but among my friends and family I spoke of LSO.

When that first rehearsal was over, it was like waking from a dream. I had pulled something off that I couldn't have done by myself. We'd made music together, rather sophisticated classical music, even if it didn't always sound so sophisticated. Magda, our conductor, left immediately after the two-hour rehearsal, but many of us spoke excitedly as we packed up our instruments. Eve introduced me to a cellist named Mary and they both urged me to also check out another adult orchestra, the Downtown Symphony, which met at the Borough of Manhattan Community College near Ground Zero. I was interested until Mary told me that I would have to audition to get in. My musical insecurities immediately resurfaced.

Audition is a scary word; it reminds me of a test. Tests freak me out. They make me feel like I will be exposed, uncovered as a fraud. I suppose that is the one A I don't relate to; the A on a test. I wasn't sure I could ace an audition.

The beauty of the Late Starters Orchestra, you see, is that there is no audition. If you think you can play with the Late Starters, you can play. You're in. The official LSO guidelines are that newcomers should have been playing their instrument "for one year." But no one checks, no one asks. And, even if they did, playing for a year can mean a lot of different things: Once a day? Once a week? Once a month? Once, period? No one asks because LSO was founded on the premise that serious music isn't only for the accomplished musician. Playing music should be accessible to all, not just the elite, not just the talented, not even just the good, but everyone. And that is what LSO practices, even if that music doesn't go much beyond the glorious A played while tuning up.

"I'm not sure I'm good enough for the Downtown Symphony," I told Eve and Mary.

"You come," Mary said, pointing her finger at me. "You may not live long enough to be 'good enough.'" Here was another twist on the late-starter philosophy emerging. At this age—and Mary had a good ten to fifteen years on me—don't put off things for tomorrow. Play now!

With Mary's words still ringing in my ears, Elena, the cofounder of the New York Late-Starters String Orchestra, announced that we had to vacate the actors' studio—we were late; our time was up—but that she was leading an expedition to the bar at the Chinese restaurant on the corner for drinks. "Join us," she said to my little group. I had promised my wife I'd be home right after rehearsal, but the chance to continue the conversation was just too enticing. I crammed myself and my cello into the elevator and made my way to Chef Yu on Eighth Avenue and Thirty-sixth

Street. It was just after five on a Sunday evening and we were welcomed warmly.

"Put your instruments there," the hostess said as she pointed to a spot near the restaurant's massive fish tank, "and take any table you want. The waiter will be right with you."

"Ah, the musicians," the waiter said a few minutes later after we unloaded our instruments and took seats around a big round table near the bar. "What can I get for the musicians?"

I've had many titles in my life—a father, a son, a husband, a reporter, an author, a professor, even a rabbi (although I am not one)—but this was a new one for me. A musician. I was tickled, even dazzled, by my new identity. But I was quickly beset by doubt. Was I really a musician? Of course I own a cello and have been trying to learn how to play it for decades, but I have never felt I was master over it. *I can see you have the soul of a musician,* I remember Mr. J telling me when we first met in 1976. *You just don't have the skills yet. We'll get you there.* That was more than three decades ago. Now, approaching sixty, was I there yet?

I ordered a beer and, ignoring the chatter around me, mused about my life.

Over my lifetime I had worked hard to reach my goals.

Everything took effort: my writing, my teaching, my friend-ships, my parenting, my faith, my marriage. What if, I wondered, I applied the same energy, commitment, and hard-work ethic to the cello as I did to everything else? Could I be good? Could I be worthy of the title musician?

I had started cello in my midtwenties under the guid-ance of a wonderful cellist named Heinrich Joachim, whom I came to call Mr. J. At the time, he was at the end of a long musical career, a career that had its dramatic ups and downs. In his prime, Mr. J, a German refugee, owned the Stradivarius of cellos, a Guarneri, and played as a solo-ist with major orchestras in the United States, Europe, and Latin America. For a decade, he was a cellist with the New York Philharmonic. By the time I met him, though, he was twice divorced and once widowed and the Guarneri was gone. He was scraping together a modest living by con-ducting a community orchestra in Westchester County, New York, and teaching adults at the going rate of thirty dollars an hour in his studio or at their homes.

Over the seven years I studied with him, he became a trusted friend and something of a father figure and was a source of valuable advice not just on music but on life. As I picked up the cello again, one of his lessons, taken from Buddhist philosophy, seemed particularly apt: *When the student is ready, the teacher will appear.* When I joined LSO, Mr. J was many years dead, but he now returned to my life in full force—and in ways that I couldn't fully appreciate when he was alive. Whether playing with LSO or practicing in my living room, Mr. J was there. He was the voice in my head and a benevolent specter in my dreams. Sometimes, I thought I could even hear his voice coming through my cello.

Right then and there, at Chef Yu on Eighth Avenue, I came up with a plan. My sixtieth birthday was approaching and I decided to see if I could live up to Mr. J's faith in me—and in the Chinese waiter's appraisal of me. I was a late starter, not once but twice. And so I decided: I would stage an elaborate birthday party to celebrate my sixtieth, and there, in front of friends and family, I would play cello in public and prove to myself—and to all of them—that I was a musician.

THE FIDDLER

If there is a character in Jewish folklore that I most relate to in my middle years, it is Tevye the Milkman from the famous story by the Yiddish writer Sholom Aleichem. Tevye is a well-meaning and lovable character who bumbles through life trying to make everyone happy—his wife, his children, his neighbors, his rabbis, his God, and even his milk cow. Tevye has certain truths he lives by—above all tradition—but he finds these truths challenged at every turn. He hears voices, imagines music, and invokes those long dead, calling on them in his sleep. His children are dragging him ever reluctantly into the future and he steps gingerly forward, his eye on the fiddler perched impossibly on his roof.

For Tevye, the fiddler represents the beauty and demands of the past, as well as the precariousness of the present. As he says in the stage version of this tale: "You might say every one of us is a fiddler on the roof, trying to scratch out a pleasant, simple tune without breaking his neck."

While Tevye is rooted in the late nineteenth century, I am rooted in the twentieth. I was born smack in the middle—in September 1949—and I am a product of the twentieth century's work ethic, its optimism and its values. Long before Ronald Reagan was president and long before I was an adult, I watched Reagan on television as a pitchman for General Electric intoning, "Progress is our most important product." I was brought up to believe that hard work would yield success and a better world.

But yet, like Tevye, I have a connection to the old world

that I hold on to for dear life. Family is precious to me, as is prayer, study, and the Sabbath day. For me, too, the fiddler represents the beauty of the past. But I didn't just want to listen to the fiddler. As I grew older, I wanted to climb up on the roof and play violin-cello duets with him. And if you think the fiddler on the roof is imperiled, imagine the cellist. His instrument is bigger and his balance even more precarious; unlike the fiddler, he needs a seat.

How does one reconcile the old and the new? Why this human desire to hold on to our roots, our foundations, even as the world all around changes rapidly? Part of us wants to preserve and protect what came before, but another, equally compelling part wants to take chances and innovate even in the face of possible failure.

For Tevye, the quest was to be "a rich man," as the song from the musical adaptation goes. But by Tevye's yardstick, we are all rich men. Cossacks are not at our door, and, despite our recent economic downturns, most of us have a "fine tin roof" over our heads and "real wooden floors below."

Baby boomers like myself sing a different tune. My song is, "If I Were a Cellist." I grew up hardly even knowing about the cello but fell in love with its sound as a young adult. It wasn't until I was twenty-six years old that

I actually held one in my hands and, thanks to the wisdom and patience of Mr. J, began to play. Since then it has been an on-again, off-again romance.

Now, I wanted to give the cello another chance in my life. Others of my generation long to reclaim their own dreams, be they on the basketball court or tennis court or on the back of a horse. There are those my age who want to learn to cook or garden or run a marathon or get on stage and act or climb aboard a motorcycle and race. For some the quest may be to build wooden scale model airplanes, for others to fly a plane, and for still others to paint landscapes.

With age, learning anything new is hard; learning a classical string instrument like the cello or violin is close to impossible. What's more, all learning needs a supportive environment. As I took up the cello once again, I found that the people in my life were skeptical.

I HAVE THE GOOD fortune of knowing the writer Elie Wiesel and he and I get together every so often to chat. I went to see him shortly after I started to play with LSO and my new quest was very much on my mind. His eyes lit up when I mentioned the cello. "I love the cello," he said. "I love the sadness of it; the richness of it."

Wiesel told me that as a boy in Hungary before the Second World War music was a central part of his life. He rhapsodized about the sounds of his youth: the Hebrew melodies of his father's synagogue, the Yiddish folk songs of his mother's kitchen, the klezmer music of a local wedding band and his own violin.

"You played the violin?" I asked in disbelief.

"Yes. One of my father's friends was teaching me to play." Wiesel had spoken before about the songs of his youth—he was even known to sing in public from time to time—but the violin? What happened to the violin?

"Juliek," he said. "After Juliek I couldn't play again."

It had been years since I read Wiesel's first book, *Night,* a heart-wrenching account of his time desperately trying to stay alive as a teenage boy trapped in a series of Nazi death camps. He writes of getting to know Juliek, a young Jew from Warsaw who was afforded special privileges in the camps because he played the violin. Macabre as it sounds, musicians such as Juliek were needed to play the marches that kept the prisoners, like Wiesel and his father, in line. Many marched to their deaths to the sounds of the band at Auschwitz.

In *Night,* Wiesel recounts that toward the end of the war, in a last desperate attempt to stay alive, he flees, taking refuge in a shed with other prisoners, some alive and some already dead. Exhausted from running all day and his foot inflamed with a painful infection, he falls off to sleep only to be awakened in the middle of the night by the tuneful sound of a violin. "The sound of a violin, in this dark shed, where the dead were heaped on the living," Wiesel writes with astonishment. "What madman could be playing the violin here, at the brink of his own grave? Or was it really an hallucination?"

When Wiesel wakes the next morning he spots the violinist Juliek, slumped over, dead. "Near him lay his violin, smashed, trampled, a strange overwhelming little corpse."

In *Night,* the smashed violin represents the death of hope. Although Wiesel survived the war and was able to rebuild his life, he told me that he could not go back to the violin. "I never played again," he said.

Wiesel and I spoke for an hour, about family, about writing, about domestic politics, about Israel, about the state of the world. In some ways, our conversation reminded me of a ritual that Mr. J and I had before our weekly lessons where we would share a cup of tea and catch up on each other's lives and on the consequential events of our time.

Afterward, Wiesel walked me to the closet of his

office and took out my coat. He held it for me. I began to slip into my coat and then realized what was happening. Wiesel, a distinguished man in his eighties, was holding my coat for me. It was such a kind and courtly gesture, one that reminded me of Mr. J.

Here is your coat, Ari, Mr. J said after our lesson. When I resisted, he would keep holding it until I relented. *When I come to your house, you can do this for me. Now you are my guest.*

There was no sense in arguing with Mr. J, but Elie Wiesel? "What are you doing?" I said. "I should be holding *your* coat!" In some ways, I was addressing both of these great men in my life.

I tried to wrest the coat from his hands but he was insistent.

Wiesel helped me with my coat.

"Thank you," I said, and then added, "I once had a cello teacher who did the same for me every week after our lesson. He was Berlin-born and half Jewish, a wonderful man and a great cellist. You remind me of him."

"I take that as a high compliment," Wiesel said with a smile. "Now, good luck with your music. But remember, Ari, you may play the cello, but you are a writer."

ANOTHER MAN MIGHT HAVE been flattered. Here was a Nobel Prize laureate and icon of his generation telling me that I was a writer. But I wasn't flattered; I was insulted. I didn't say it, but I thought it: *Why do you assume that I am only a writer? Maybe I'm also a musician. How do you know I'm not a cellist? Did you ever hear me play?*

"I've heard you play," my wife, Shira, told me that night when I repeated what Wiesel had said. "And, sweetheart, you are not a musician."

Shira is a most supportive wife. But she also won't allow me to wallow in my illusions. I was studying with Mr. J when Shira and I first started dating in 1983. She saw my love for the instrument—and the man. But she had also watched my cello obsession wax and wane over the decades of our marriage. I clearly hadn't convinced her that my latest infatuation with LSO was any different from earlier attempts to master the instrument.

After Mr. J died, I tried out other teachers but none of them had the faith in me that he did.

After I committed to performing at my birthday party, I turned to a teacher named Noah Hoffeld, a versatile young cellist whose repertoire ranged well beyond the classical.

Noah was more likely to play in rock clubs, churches, and synagogues than concert halls. He was laid-back and easy-going. His music studio was like a Zen retreat center with busts of the Buddha and burning candles and incense. But he could also dish out some tough love.

"Ari, you've plateaued," Noah told me after working with me on and off for almost a year. He spoke about other adult students he had who never missed a day of practice and who kept improving. "I can't continue to teach you unless you try harder, much harder." I was shocked at his strident tone. After all, I was paying him handsomely—and he was going to drop me? I assured him that I was practicing, although practicing is one of those things you can never seem to do enough of.

"Ari, I expect more," he said sternly.

I started playing every night. Some nights it was just fifteen or twenty minutes and some nights longer but not much longer, except on the weekends, when I had more time and could play during the day. My commitment was to at least hold the cello every night. *You can't even begin to call yourself a musician unless you play every day,* Mr. J said.

With practice, my cello playing improved but not my relationship with our neighbors. We live in a sturdy one-hundred-year-old apartment building on a busy avenue in

New York City just a block from Columbia University, where I teach. The apartment has thick walls and high ceilings, but a cello can sound rather loud especially late at night when the traffic on the street slows down. Our neighbor András complained. I didn't know much about András. I knew he was from Hungary and that he and his wife had two small children (we saw them in the elevator). We knew he ran marathons (we saw him dashing through the park) but that was about it. They were extremely quiet people. We never heard a peep out of them—no music, no singing, no raised voices—and it seemed that they expected the same from us.

We, however, are a volatile bunch, a lot like Tevye's clan in Anatevka. Music, singing, and raised voices are just the beginning. Arguing, fighting, and debating—all good-natured, of course—are common in our house. We have no milk cow, but we do have two Pomeranians, Alfie and Nala, who can get pretty yappy at times. András had at times complained about our upright piano, which our son Adam played with abandon in his youth, but he seemed especially sensitive to my cello playing. András would often call the house to ask us to keep it down. He got so annoying that we stopped answering the phone. Then he took to climbing the flight of stairs between us and knocked on our door. "Can you keep it down? Do you know what time it is?" András was standing there in his pajamas. I often wondered if András would complain if I was any good at the cello. After all, it wasn't that late. Maybe it wasn't the hour but the music?

My children were far more tolerant of my cello playing, but I had a feeling that they were not fully convinced of my abilities. I told them I needed their forbearance just a little while longer. "Let me get to my sixtieth birthday. If I can't play by then, I'll give it up."

Adam, who moved to Germany after college to start a writing career, asked Shira during one of their marathon Skype conversations, "Is Dad really going to subject everybody to his cello playing at his birthday party?" Adam wasn't a roll-your-eyes-at-Dad teen. He was twenty-five and making a living as a freelance music writer and opera critic in Berlin. He knew good music . . . and bad.

My daughter, Emma, took a gentler approach. "Dad, you have such a nice voice. Why don't you sing some folk songs at your party?" Emma was twenty-one and a college junior who had just given up as a voice major and turned to philosophy. She had to stop singing because she developed polyps on her vocal cords. But she loved music more than ever.

The only one who believed in me was my fourteen-year-old son Judah, himself a cellist. "It's really not hard, Dad. You can do it." Of course, it was easy for Judah. He'd been playing cello since he was six years old and was damn good at it. When I thought about it, the whole thing didn't make much sense. Judah had been playing for eight years and I'd been playing—off and on—for thirty-five. So why was he so good and I wasn't?

JUDAH HAS THE MOST important advantage for any musician—youth. It's not just that learning is easier and the fingers move quicker, it's the brain. As the neurologist and psychiatrist Oliver Sacks explains in his book *Musicophilia,* people who learn music at a young age actually grow a set of brain neurons that we late starters simply don't have and will never have. Modern brain-imaging studies have enabled scientists to visualize the brains of musicians and to compare them with those of nonmusicians. "The corpus callosum, the great commissure that connects the two hemispheres of the brain," Sacks writes, "is enlarged in professional musicians." Were the musicians just born with these bigger musical brains or were they developed over time? Sacks wonders. He cites studies that conclude "beyond dispute" that the brain of a person given intensive musical training at a young age develops differently from that of someone without musical training. "The effects of such training," Sacks concludes, "are very great." The anatomical changes, he adds, quoting the results of one popular study, "were strongly correlated with the age at which musical training began and with the intensity of practice and rehearsal."

Norman Doidge in his outstanding study *The Brain That Changes Itself* is even more pointed. Doidge, a psychiatrist and psychoanalyst, writes: "Brain imaging shows that musicians have several areas of their brains—the motor cortex and the cerebellum, among others—that differ from those of nonmusicians. Imaging also shows that musicians who begin playing before the age of seven have larger brain areas connecting the two hemispheres."

In short: the earlier you start and the more intensive practice you have under your belt, the bigger your "musical brain."

The ancient Jewish sources that I studied as a youngster corroborate Sack's scientific findings. What you learn as a child sticks with you, says the Talmud, the library of Jewish lore and law. I guess I remember that one because I learned it as a kid.

The odds were stacked against me. I was in my late

fifties, my musical brain was puny, and many of the people around me thought I was crazy. "Don't you have better things to do?" a few of them asked. I had a wife and three children, one in college, one in middle school, and one living abroad on his own. I also had a bad back—a ruptured disk on the third vertebra to be exact—and it went out every so often, making tying my shoes, let alone toting and playing a large instrument, a challenge. And I was a professor of journalism, with an ever-renewing cohort of students and a growing number of former students, many of whom were panicked about their jobs or prospects for employment in the increasingly unstable field of journalism.

My profession was undergoing the greatest upheaval since Gutenberg invented movable type almost six hundred years earlier. The Internet had changed everything, from how news is gathered to how it is consumed. The authoritative names in news like the *Washington Post* and CBS were being replaced by Yahoo and Google and the *Huffington Post* and other outlets that didn't even exist a few years earlier. The *New York Times,* where I worked for twenty years before coming to teach at Columbia, was laying off reporters and editors. Newspapers around the country were cutting back their operations or simply folding.

The newspaper business that I grew up with was becoming the news business. In my youth if you didn't read the newspapers, you tuned into the evening news. But almost no one was watching them anymore, either. I remember gathering around the television after dinner to watch Walter Cronkite assure us that "that's the way it is." Instead, television viewers had migrated to the opinion-laden and endless talk shows of Fox and MSNBC. Instead of "that's the way it is," we were hearing "that's the way we want it to be." Young people were getting their news from Jon Stewart and Stephen Colbert on Comedy Central. Books were rapidly being replaced by handheld electronic devices called Kindle and Nook. The growth of e-books was so steady that many predicted that old-fashioned paper books would soon disappear.

On top of all that, the economy was tanking in the year I was turning sixty. The venerable investment house of Lehman Brothers had declared bankruptcy the year before and the government was faced with the decision of either letting other businesses, especially the auto industry, go under or trying to shore them up with government bailouts.

There was much to do and so much to say, both in my private life and in my professional life. There were classes to teach, parties and dinners to attend, books to read, movies and museum exhibitions to see, and a rich religious life to explore.

But all I wanted to do was play the cello, formally called the violoncello, an instrument that was beginning to take its modern shape in Gutenberg's time.

THE CELLO

The music that Tevye heard—or thought he heard—came from a fiddle, which is pretty much just another name for the violin. What's the difference between a violin and a fiddle? One Irish folk musician I know put it this way: "A fiddle is a violin with an attitude." Fiddling refers more to the style of music than the instrument itself. It is used for jigs and reels, while the violin is used for symphonies, concertos, and sonatas. People sit when they listen to a violin; they dance when they hear a fiddle. And just as you can fiddle on a violin, you can fiddle on a cello. Yo-Yo Ma, probably the most famous classical cellist of our time and known for his mastery of the classical music repertoire, has gone the fiddling route more than a few times to record with folk, jazz, and Celtic musicians.

What's the difference between a violin and a cello?

Here, it's more than simply attitude. The cello is easily three times the size of the violin. Given its bigger body and thicker strings, the cello produces a much lower sound. It is held vertically, between the legs, rather than horizontally under the chin like a violin.

In musical history, the violin came first. It dates back to the late twelfth and early thirteenth centuries and its sound reflects the fashion of the day. Ideal sound of the early middle ages was high-pitched, whiny, and nasal, not unlike traditional Asian and Indian music. The violin was designed with the female musical voice in mind.

But around 1450, composers sought a lower range, not so much to be played by a solo instrument, but as a lower-register—or bass—accompaniment to the high-pitched voice and violin. Bass parts began to appear with some regularity in musical notation. The cello as we know it—bigger, fuller, more robust in sound than the violin—began to take shape. The viola da braccio, as a smaller and earlier version of the cello was called, was cradled under the chin, but it was soon moved down to the ground and held between the legs. These early cellos rested on the ground when played, or they were clasped between the player's calves or were supported by a string roped around the player's neck. It was much later, in the eighteen hundreds, when a peg or "end pin" was added to lift the instrument a foot or so off the floor.

The first known cello maker was Andrea Amati (1520–1578) of Cremona, Italy, a luthier who made elaborately decorated cellos for the court of the French king, Charles IX. Amati's was a family business and he passed his skills on to his sons, Antonio and Girolamo. The greatest of the Amatis was Andrea's grandson, Nicolò, who practiced and taught the luthier art to many, including Antonio Stradivari (1644–1737) and Andrea Guarneri (1626–1698).

Both Stradivari and Guarneri went on to found their own workshops in Italy, where, working with their children and other trained craftsmen, they continued to perfect the art of violin and cello making. If some of the most famous violins that survive today bear the name Stradivarius, some of the most renowned cellos are Guarneris. Mr. J bought his Guarneri, which was made in 1669, for ten thousand dollars when he first came to New York from Guatemala in 1946. Pretty expensive back then, but nothing like it would cost later when the price of antique classical instruments skyrocketed. *Smooth, satiny, and delicate in tone,* Mr. J recalled, lovingly. But it proved to be more suited for chamber music than the concert stage. As Mr. J's career advanced, and he was being invited to play with major orchestras, he needed a cello that was a stronger solo instrument. Around 1970, he sold the Guarneri to David Soyer, the founding cellist of the Guarneri String Quartet, for thirty thousand dollars. Mr. J bought a cello made by another luthier, Domenico Montagnana, who made cellos in Italy in the early seventeen hundreds. It was a mighty and robust instrument that had a big sound suited for the great concert halls. But it was not particularly suited for Mr. J. He came to regard it as too big. He eventually sold it and sought to buy back the Guareneri, but by then it was well out of his price range. Mr. J's son Andrew told me that Soyer wanted three hundred thousand dollars for it just a few years later.

According to Margaret Campbell's sweeping history of the instrument, *The Great Cellists,* cellos reached a state of perfection during this Italian period. Owing to the choice of woods and the shape, master craftsmen like Stradivari and Guarneri created instruments that amplified the vibration of the strings without favoring some notes at the expense of others. Aside from the introduction of the end pin—added by a particularly corpulent cellist, Adrien François Servais of Belgium (1807–1866), who had trouble managing the instrument between his legs—little else about the cello has changed in the past two hundred years.

For all its tonal and physical beauty, Campbell writes, the cello was for a very long time relegated to a subsidiary role in public performance. Cellists were invited into chapels and theaters to accompany singers; only occasionally were they invited to play short preludes or incidental music. According to one church instruction given them in the sixteen hundreds, they were to be "modest therein," using ornamentation only "at the proper time and with taste." Among the first to write music for cello was the Italian Baroque composer Antonio Vivaldi of Venice (1678–1741), who is probably most famous for his work *The Four Seasons,* still a concert staple of the string orchestra. While he composed hundreds of works for the violin, he also wrote twenty-seven pieces that highlighted the beauty of the cello. He wrote these in particular for the young ladies of the Ospedale della Pietà, the convent, orphanage, and music school where Vivaldi, a Catholic priest, taught. The Pietà would periodically opens its doors for public concerts throughout the seventeenth century. The young women would sing Vivaldi's music and some would play cello and other instruments.

The first cello celebrity was a contemporary of Vivaldi, Francesco Alborea of Naples (1691–1739), the Yo-Yo Ma of his day. He was so closely associated with the instrument that he became known throughout Europe as "Franciscello." He toured Europe, drawing audiences never before imagined for an instrument that had so long been relegated to secondary, "accompaniment" status.

The person who combined both the virtuosity of Franciscello and the great composing gifts of Vivaldi was Luigi Boccherini (1743–1805). Born in Lucca, Italy, Boccherini picked up where they left off. Boccherini started playing cello at five and made his first concert appearance at thirteen. At seventeen, he completed a set of six trios for two violins and cello that became his opus 1, the first of hundreds. His most enduring work in the modern repertoire is his Cello Concerto no. 9.

Boccherini quite literally pushed the cello to new musical heights, Mr. J told me. He demonstrated by showing me "thumb position" on his cello. He shifted his left hand from behind the neck of the cello to higher registers of the fingerboard, pressed down firmly on the strings, and then proceeded to explore the full soprano range of the cello that Boccherini opened up. *I'm playing the cello,* Mr. J said, *but you are hearing the violin.*

Although Boccherini produced some of the most gorgeous music for the cello, he remains one of the instrument's tragic figures. He was recognized as a prodigy and was celebrated in the courts of Europe, picking up patrons and commissions as he went. In 1771, at the age of twenty-eight, he married Clementina Pelicho, who bore him five children but who died of a stroke a few years later. Then his patron, Infante Don Luis, died. But his troubles weren't over. Next, his publisher, in whom he had entrusted all his compositions, stole all his royalties and commissions. When Boccherini's two daughters died within a few days of each other from an epidemic in 1802, his biographer said that he seemed to lose all will to live. He died despondent and impoverished in 1805 at the age of sixty-two.

The next great pivotal figure in the history of the cello, Pablo Casals (1876–1973), lived a happier and much longer life. If Boccherini expanded the instrument's possibilities with the orchestra, Casals elevated it as never before as a solo instrument.

Casals was born in the Catalonia region of Spain, the son of the local church organist and his wife, a former music student of the organist who had emigrated from Puerto Rico. As a boy, Casals exhibited considerable musical talent—he sang in the church choir at five—but his father, Carlos, feared that Pablo would never make a living as a musician. He made plans to apprentice him to a carpenter. However, the boy's mother, Pilar, insisted that he study music. "She was convinced that I had a special gift and that everything should be done to nourish it," Casals wrote in his autobiography *Joys and Sorrows*. Although he played piano, flute, and violin at a very early age, he never even saw a cello until a group of traveling musicians came to his village. One of them played the cello. In his book, Casals recalls rushing home and breathlessly telling his father about the strange instrument. His father made him a cello out of a hollowed-out gourd strung with a single string. "On that homemade contrivance I learned to play many of the songs my father wrote, as well as popular melodies that reached our village from the outer world," Casals wrote.

When he was eleven, his mother took him by train to Barcelona to enroll him in the municipal music school. His parents visited him regularly and one memorable time, when Pablo was thirteen, they stopped at an old music shop near the harbor and browsed through the sheet music. "Suddenly," Casals wrote, "I came upon a sheaf of pages, crumbled and discolored with age. They were the unaccompanied suites by Johann Sebastian Bach—for cello only!"

The Bach suites were a little-known collection considered to be musical exercises for students and seen as unfit to play in public. But not for Casals. For the rest of his life, Casals devoted himself to these Bach suites and, through his public performances and recordings, eventually assured them the same stature as Bach's famous work for piano, *The Well-Tempered Clavier.* In 1904, Casals was invited to play for President Theodore Roosevelt in the White House, and he was invited back in 1961 to play for President John F. Kennedy.

Casals was known also as a conductor and as early as 1919, he organized an orchestra in Barcelona, but with the outbreak of the Spanish Civil War in 1936, he left Spain. He was an ardent supporter of the Spanish Republican government, and, after its defeat by the forces loyal to Francisco Franco, Casals vowed not to return to Spain until democracy was restored. He lived out the rest of his life in exile, first in France and later in Puerto Rico, the birthplace of his mother. He died there in 1973 at the age of ninety-six. Several years later, after the end of the Franco regime, Casals was honored by the Spanish government under King Juan Carlos. His remains were reinterred in his native Catalonia.

I was inspired by stories of the great cellists of the past and I began to consume their biographies and listen to their music. Vivaldi, Franciscello, Boccherini, and Casals were only the beginning. I explored the lives of Jacqueline du Pré, the gifted cellist struck down at the height of her career by multiple sclerosis; the Russian cellist Mstislav Rostropovich, whose Soviet citizenship was revoked in the 1970s because of his campaign for human rights; and Vedran Smailovic, who became known as "the cellist of Sarajevo" for playing his cello in the center of the city as the Bosnian War raged around him. And there was no escaping the music and life story of the versatile Yo-Yo Ma.

Study the greats and you can become great, Mr. J said.

But the more I followed his advice and explored these great cellists, the more I was curious about Mr. J himself. As I approached sixty, I believed he still had many lessons to teach me. And, judging by how often I heard his voice, so did he.

THE CELLO, WHICH GREW in status and thrived as an instrument in the twentieth century, seemed to be in danger of losing its resonance in the twenty-first. Or so I feared. In an era in which computers, laptops, and smartphones rule, an instrument like the cello is the ultimate throwback. It has no wires and it has no memory. It is just a lot of wood and four strings made of metal and catgut and a bow made of wood and horsehair. In the right hands, though, it has a rich, sad, and soulful sound like nothing else in God's creation. In his book *Cello Story,* the cellist Dimitry Markevitch writes that the cello "allow[s] one to express the most profound feelings, to convey emotions that stir the soul, and yet to give a sensation of total peace."

I wanted to play like that.

And to do so I had to come up with a strategy. This wasn't going to happen without a lifestyle change. After I joined LSO, I resolved to spend all my free time practicing. That meant ignoring my neighbor András. It also meant no more going to the gym or walking in the park. "I don't care if I get fat," I told myself, "I must learn how to play." People tell me that I give a slim appearance—when I have my clothes on. But when I am home alone and stepping out of the shower, I can see the effects of the years of sitting at a typewriter and then a computer keyboard. I have little muscle tone on my upper body and my center of gravity has shifted to my stomach.

But I had to rethink my priorities. At this stage in my life, I realized that building my musical brain was more important than building my pecs or flattening my abs. The time I would spend at the gym, I decided, I would spend instead with the cello.

The second step was even more radical. I have eclectic tastes in music and have a collection on my iPod that ranges from folk to rock to jazz to classical to what has become known as "world music." The sounds include Latin, African, Caribbean, Egyptian, French, Israeli, and Hasidic music. Sometimes I just put my iPod on shuffle and am surprised by what comes up: Dylan, Edith Piaf, 10,000 Maniacs, Yo-Yo Ma, Joan Baez, Shlomo Carlebach, Dave Brubeck, Vivaldi, Alison Krauss, even an aria from Mozart's *Don Giovanni* or Puccini's *Tosca*. But if I wanted to be a cellist, I reasoned, I had to focus on cello music. I went out and bought all the Casals, Rostropovich, du Pré, and Ma I could find. Then I erased everything else. I highlighted so much of my beloved music and pressed "delete," "delete," "delete" again and again. It was downright painful. But I had a purpose. I dedicated myself to listening to the great cellists in a new way, trying to understand what it was about their playing that set them apart and made them great. I wanted to train my ear to know greatness. I wanted to absorb whatever lessons they had to offer.

My third step was to devote my Sunday afternoons to LSO. There is only so much time you can spend in your teacher's music studio or in your living room practicing scales. Even Mr. J, who upheld the discipline of regular practice as the highest value, knew it had its limitations.

Music is not a solitary pursuit. You need melody—and you need harmony. And, ultimately, you need an audience.

Finding LSO had been a stroke of good luck. New York is not the kind of town that has too many orchestras for a perpetual novice. It is a city of perfectionists, at least when it comes to music. New York is where the greats come to play—the most accomplished orchestras, the most talented soloists play here—and, if they rate, the press heralds their "New York debut." It is not a place for mediocrity. To be sure, there are a few community orchestras, but they tend to be for the elite amateurs who may have dropped out of conservatory to go to medical school or work on Wall Street. Such places would have no interest in the likes of me.

But LSO did. The Late Starters Orchestra is a spinoff of a movement that started in Europe in the 1980s with the East London Late Starters and continued with the movement's bastard child, the Really Terrible Orchestra of Edinburgh, two organizations committed to the notion that everyone should have a place to make music.

Listening to cello music, playing with LSO once a week, studying with Noah, and rehearsing by myself each night was a good start, but it still did not suffice. As my birthday approached, I decided to spend one week at an adult music camp in Maine, near the Canadian border, and another week at a summer music retreat in the north of England run by our sister orchestra, the East London Late Starters.

I did not change overnight, of course. I learned that there are no overnight sensations, especially when you are my age. But I noticed one important thing as my birthday approached: I was getting better, not by leaps and bounds, but by small, almost imperceptible steps. No one else noticed, it seemed; not my wife, not my older children, not András, but I could see the difference. I had greater command of the bow, I was hitting the right notes on the fingerboard, my timing improved, my vibrato resonated. I was now something more than just *musical.* I was becoming a *musician.*

PART TWO

OVERTURES

There are two things that don't have to mean anything;
one is music, the other is laughter.

—IMMANUEL KANT

If the people in my immediate circle were skeptical, I found encouragement from the words and examples of other late starters. Eve, with whom I sat that first day in the Late Starters Orchestra, stood five feet, one inch tall and wore her hair in a pageboy cut that shook and flopped around like a white mop when she played. Cello was not her first instrument; in fact she did not pick it up until she was in her late sixties.

Eve grew up in Philadelphia. There was a piano in the house, but that was the instrument of her older brother, so, wanting to be different, she took up the flute and played through high school and college. She also sang in choruses and spent two summers of her youth singing at the summer music festival in Tanglewood, the summer home of the Boston Symphony Orchestra.

Eve didn't marry until she was thirty (she was a "late starter" to marriage, too, she joked, especially back in the 1960s). In fact, she and her husband met in an amateur orchestra. She played flute, he the trombone. But music took a backseat in her life as she raised three children and worked as a proofreader and secretary for organizations that she believed in, like the ACLU. Later, she worked in her husband's photo print shop.

With her children out of the house and the shop closed, Eve's thoughts returned to music. "One day I was walking by the Third Street Music School and saw this sign that read: NEW CELLO CLASS FOR ADULT BEGINNERS. LIMITED TO THREE STUDENTS.

"To be honest, I was always terrified of the cello," she told me, explaining that she found "daunting" the notion of carrying it around and tuning its four strings. "But I figured I should confront my fears. . . . So I walked in and signed up. They even supplied me with a cello." It was not a natural fit. The cello was big for her small frame, but Eve compensated by moving around the instrument more like a double bass player in a jazz quintet than a cellist in an orchestra.

She picked it up at sixty-seven and still hadn't let go a decade later. From what I could see, in those ten years she had achieved something extraordinary. In ensembles, you don't often hear your fellow musicians playing individually. It's one of the aspects that I like about it. You can hide and even get lost in the crowd. You are in an orchestra but you've got cover. Every so often, though, a cello solo is called for and, for that, the first cellist takes center stage. One day at rehearsal, we were playing a short, upbeat, dance-like piece by the Norwegian composer Edvard Grieg called "From Holberg's Time," a composition written in the nineteenth century meant to evoke the eighteenth. As often happens, the violins carry the melody at first and then it shifts to the cellos or more precisely one cello. The cello ensemble is instructed in the music to "pizz," which means to pluck strings in what is properly called pizzicato. My fellow section cellists and I were plinking, while one cello—Eve's—began to intone the melody. It took my breath away.

I dared not play with her, but I sang along with her melody, quietly and under my breath.

If rhythm emerges from the body, melody springs from the voice, Mr. J would say. *Everything is a melody, even a baby's cry. It may start with a whimper and escalate to a screech. But then the baby finds the mother's breast and a gentle cooing is heard. Of course, the baby doesn't know he's singing,*

but he is. He doesn't know he is in the middle of a drama—a
grand opera, perhaps—but he is. Think of melody as a plot,
a tale of love or conflict or struggle. Melody tells a story.

When I heard Eve play, I heard the melody but I also
heard her story, the story of a late starter who, to my ears,
played like an early starter. How did she become that
good? After the rehearsal, I asked Eve about the place of
music in her life. "What does your typical week look like?"
I asked her. Maybe if I followed her model, I could play
like that, too.

I was astonished to learn that music wasn't a side dish
for Eve, but the actual main course of her life. Indeed, she
was actively engaged in playing every single day. Her week
was all music, all the time:

Sunday: The Late Starters Orchestra
Monday: Amateur Chamber Music at the 92nd Street Y
Tuesday: The Downtown Symphony
Wednesday: Cello lessons with Allen Sher, formerly of
    the Pittsburgh Symphony Orchestra
Thursday: Trombone lessons at the Third Street Music
    School Settlement
Friday: More coached chamber music at the 92nd Street
    Y, these sessions specifically for those sixty or over
Saturday: Practice, practice, practice.

It all made sense, except Thursday.

"Trombone lessons?" I asked.

"I couldn't resist," Eve said with a smile.

THE NEXT CHAPTER

What Eve was experiencing in her late seventies—and what I was beginning to feel in my late fifties—is part of a much larger trend. Simply put, people are living longer, and, with leisure time increasing and jobs disappearing, often have more time on their hands. Over the course of the twentieth century, life expectancy in America rose from an average of just over forty-nine years to seventy-seven and a half years. The baby boomers (those born between 1946 and 1964—my generation), the twentieth century's noisiest and most demanding generation, are now moving into their sixties and their quest for learning, meaning, growth, and attention is unabated. American universities are increasingly catering to this population by opening up their classrooms and offering special nondegree programs to the boomer set. Sociologists have a variety of names for the transition into this phase of life.

Sara Lawrence-Lightfoot, a Harvard sociologist, calls it "the third chapter" and writes about it in a book by that name. She tells the stories of people who, late in life, are learning to speak a foreign language, play jazz piano, surf, act, and write plays. What characterizes them all, she writes, is "the willingness to take risks, experience vulnerability and uncertainty, learn from experimentation and failure, seek guidance and counsel from younger generations, and develop new relationships of support and intimacy."

Patricia Cohen, the author of *In Our Prime: The Invention of Middle Age,* believes that education is the key. Discussing a brain study conducted by two psychologists at Brandeis University, Cohen writes, "For those in midlife and beyond, a college diploma subtracted a decade from one's brain age."

Music is even better. I can hear Mr. J saying. *It shaves twenty years off brain age.* Rhythm springs from the body and melody from the voice. But harmony, he taught me, springs from the mind. *To find harmony we must find balance. It is about constantly making judgments. Above all, harmony is exercise for the mind.*

Several studies show that musicians tend to remain sharper in old age than those who do not have music in their lives. Those with musical training outperformed nonmusicians in both visual and verbal memory tasks. It wasn't only in aural memory that they exceeded the others; it was also in remembering what they read and saw as well. Those who started musical training young had a greater advantage, but even late starters did better than nonmusicians in memory tasks.

In one study, conducted at the University of Kansas, researchers compared three groups of seventy healthy older adults ranging in age from sixty to eighty-three. They divided their subjects into three groups: nonmusicians, low-activity musicians (one to nine years of musical training), and high-activity musicians (ten years or more). The researchers did their best to control for every possible condition of importance, including intelligence, physical activity, and education. Still, the results showed that the more music, the better the memory, the quicker the processing speed, and the more adroit the cognitive flexibility. Music, it seemed, was able to take an eighty-year-old mind and turn it into a mind more befitting of a sixty-year-old.

You can read about the benefits of adult learning in such places as *Psychology Today,* a magazine where the median age of readers is forty-five. (One recent *Psychology Today* feature article had this headline: MUSIC LESSONS: THEY'RE NOT JUST FOR KIDS ANYMORE.) And, of course, music isn't the only way to sharpen the mind. There are also numerous inspirational books on the market touting the value of any kind of lifelong learning, books with the titles *Aging Well, The Art of Aging, From Age-ing to Sage-ing,* and this one with a cautionary title, *The Denial of Aging: Perpetual Youth, Eternal Life, and Other Dangerous Fantasies.* Magazines like *AARP* often feature stories about actors, writers, and painters who come to their craft late in life. Julia Child did not even know how to cook until her late thirties; Grandma Moses didn't pick up a paintbrush until she was in her seventies; Tillie Olsen published her first book at forty-nine; Danny Aiello didn't act until he was forty. However, in all these compilations, there is no list of great classical musicians who start late.

Guitarists, yes, but cellists, no.

In his book *Guitar Zero,* Gary Marcus writes about his personal quest to learn guitar as he approaches his fortieth birthday. Marcus, a psychologist, takes comfort in the stories of rock stars who came relatively late to their craft, like Patti Smith, who didn't seriously consider singing until her midtwenties; and Tom Morello, who didn't pick up a guitar until his late teens.

At thirty-eight, Marcus knew that the cards were stacked against him but he believed that he could master the guitar. "I wanted to know whether I could overcome my intrinsic limits, my age, my lack of talent," he writes. In the course of the book, he actually becomes quite competent on the guitar.

Marcus also revels in the ignorance of many famous guitarists when it comes to reading music. "None of the Beatles could read or write music," Marcus notes, "and neither can Eric Clapton."

It's a good thing none of them played a classical string instrument. Cello is different. An ability to read music is required and there is no greatness unless you start young. Very young. "A string player should begin at 5," the great violinist Alexander Schneider said. "Later is too late."

ORIGINS

When I was five, string instruments were the farthest thing from my life. On the eve of my sixth birthday, my mother left my father in Hartford, Connecticut, and I began a new life with her and my two brothers in a small apartment in the Jackson Heights section of Queens, New York. Her leaving was the first salvo in a divorce proceeding that was to drag on for a good part of my childhood. For me, my parents' separation and eventual divorce meant geographic dislocation, emotional and financial hardship, and family dissention that, quite remarkably, lasts to this day, even though my parents are long gone from this earth.

The one bright spot in my young life was music. I sang. I sang on the streets and I sang in school and I sang on the subway and I sang in bed and I sang in the synagogue. I had a remarkably good, clear, and energetic voice, one with distinct timbre, flexibility, and range.

It was very important to my father that I sing in the synagogue. Music, the music of the synagogue, was a link that kept us close even as I moved away and saw him only on weekends and holidays. My father wanted me to use my gift for the glory of God. From the time I was very young, he trained me to sing the solos that a small child can lead, such as the concluding hymns of "Aleynu" and "Adon Olam." And, most of all, he trained me for my bar mitzvah, the day that I would be able to lead the adult congregation in prayer.

On the weekends that I spent with my father in Hartford, we would rise early Saturday mornings to attend synagogue. As Orthodox Jews, we did not take the car, no matter how hot or cold the weather. We walked in winter snowstorms and in spring rain showers. In traditional Judaism, to ride in the comfort of your car is a violation of the Sabbath, but to walk in terrible weather is fine; a mitzvah, even. Outside of traditional Judaism, our walks might not make much sense, but I wouldn't have traded that time with my dad for anything. As we made our way to synagogue, about a ten-minute-long stroll, we held hands and sang. My dad would have me practice the special songs for Shabbat and we would talk excitedly about how we could innovate with extra melodies and vocal flourishes. Our voices resounded through the early morning streets.

I was loud for a little kid and could even project in Orthodox synagogues, which, in keeping with traditional Jewish law, did not use a microphone on the Sabbath. My bar mitzvah, held at the Orthodox Young Israel of Jackson Heights in Queens, New York, in late 1962, was a festival of song—with me as the star. Most bar mitzvah boys—there were no bat mitzvah girls in Orthodox synagogues in those days—read the Torah portion (a selection from the Five Books of Moses) and the Haftorah (additional selections from the Prophets). My voice was so good and renowned in our little circle that I was allowed to take over the whole service. I led the morning prayers, *Shacharit,* and the so-called "additional service," *Musaf,* incorporating melodies both traditional and new. I sang songs inspired by the young State of Israel and by Hasidic melodies, especially as interpreted by the singing rabbi of that era, Rabbi Shlomo Carlebach. I even incorporated some of the vocal techniques and inflections I had learned from my folk heroes. One friend told me I sounded like I was auditioning for the Kingston Trio.

Without a banjo, of course. There were no musical instruments on the Sabbath either. No banjos and certainly no cellos. The Bible is sparing in its references to instruments, most of which were played to honor festivals and kings and to accompany the sacred service in the ancient Temple. The *Encyclopedia Judaica* lists nineteen instruments referenced in the Bible, including the lyre, the lute, the recorder, the harp, and a variety of horns, drums, and bells. Psalm 150 includes a veritable orchestra. "Praise God in his sanctuary," the psalm begins. "Praise him with the sound of the shofar, praise him with the harp and the lyre. Praise him with the timbrel and dance, praise him with stringed instruments and the pipe. Praise him upon sounding cymbals, praise him with loud crashing cymbals."

The harp and the lyre were used in the ancient Temple on the Sabbath, but after the destruction of the Temple in 70 CE and the dispersal of the Jews into exile, the rabbis forbade their use on the Sabbath and were even ambivalent about music during the rest of the week. The nation of Israel was in mourning, the rabbis declared, and celebrations should be toned down. Music was still played at weddings, but even Jewish weddings are famously muted, even to this day. That is why a glass is broken. Even at our happiest moments, part of us is still in mourning for the loss of the Temple.

And why not? Even the wedding scene in *Fiddler on the Roof* is broken up by the arrival of the Cossacks. It is a most happy day when, despite Tevye's initial plan, his daughter Tzeitel marries Motel the Tailor. The scene begins with the sentimental "Sunrise, Sunset" and ends with the exuberant "Wedding Celebration and Bottle Dance." And then, at the height of the celebration, the Cossacks arrive and upend Anatevka. Unrestrained joy is not part of Jewish culture.

The "classical" music of my youth meant one thing: the music of the synagogue. I didn't know of Bach or Beethoven. I knew how to chant the Torah and Haftorah, ancient books that had their own musical notation and strict rules. Every word, for example, had an assigned note. Miss a note or, worse, miss a word, and the entire reading was flawed, so flawed in some cases the reading had to be done all over again. Folk music was my rebellion. It provided a relief from all that rigor and precision and allowed for easy harmonies and quick innovation. The folk musicians I loved—Pete Seeger, Woody Guthrie, Tom Paxton, Joan Baez, Judy Collins, Joni Mitchell, early Bob Dylan and, above all, Phil Ochs—wrote and sang right from the headlines. Their music was fresh and inventive (even if it occasionally all sounded the same) and broke all the rules. It shaped not only my musical tastes but my social consciousness.

I attended an all-boys ultra-Orthodox high school in Brooklyn that did its best to wall us off from the corrupting influences of modern society, but the outside world inevitably seeped in. If I gave the Beatles little attention when they first came to America in 1964, it wasn't because I was so immersed in the study of Talmud. It was because the British imports seemed downright frivolous singing "I Want to Hold Your Hand" and "I Saw Her Standing There" when there was a war going on in Vietnam and race riots in the South. I was captivated instead by the folksingers who were fighting for peace, racial equality, and the rights of workers. Soon after my bar mitzvah in 1962, I picked up a guitar, mindful of the words scrawled on Woody Guthrie's guitar, "THIS MACHINE KILLS FAS-CISTS." I sang Ochs's "I Ain't Marching Anymore," Dylan's "Blowin' in the Wind," and Guthrie's "Union Maid." My friend Marty, a fellow yeshiva rebel, and I would take our guitars to Washington Square Park and sing our hearts out, not for the coins people tossed in our beat-up guitar cases but to feel a part of the revolution happening all around us. Marty was by far the stronger guitarist, but I had the voice. He strummed and I sang.

And then something terrible happened. My voice changed. After my sixteenth birthday, I couldn't reach the high notes—or the low notes—and the middle range was uninspired. At first, I tried to ignore it and continued to sing my heart out, but others noticed. I was passed over for honors in the synagogue. And Marty found another singing partner.

I put down the guitar and avoided the synagogue spotlight. The voice that had given me so much pleasure—and earned me so much attention and approval—was gone. I put all my energies in high school and college into my next favorite thing: writing. While at college at Yeshiva University, I discovered the student newspaper and found I loved newspapers almost as much as I loved music. I read the daily paper voraciously. I dreamed about it at night, even imagining that I was scanning the columns of the next day's edition. Those were my rapid eye movements. I wanted nothing more in the world than to become a newspaper reporter. In college I wrote an article about the *New York Times* campus correspondent at Yeshiva, a senior named Harry Weiss. In the piece, I explained how the *Times,* eager to know what was going on on campuses around the country, had put together a network of campus correspondents, called "stringers," and how Yeshiva became one of them. When Harry graduated, he made me the stringer at Yeshiva.

At nineteen, I had my toe in the door of the *Times* and I didn't let the door close for the next two decades. I went from being a stringer to a copy boy—the lowest editorial job in the newsroom and one that hardly exists anymore because of technology—to news clerk to news assistant to reporter trainee to reporter. I had numerous beats, but I hardly ever wrote about music, nor was it much on my agenda, that is, until one day, quite by accident, I ran into an irresistible musician who taught cello.

I was, at the time, a newly minted reporter in the newspaper's Long Island bureau and on my way to an interview in an old office building when I knocked on the wrong door. A short, stocky man with a beautiful shock of white hair came to the door rubbing sleep from his eyes. The room behind him was dark but the light from the hallway illuminated a most beautiful wooden cello case behind him.

Forgetting why I knocked in the first place, I asked, "Do you play the cello?"

"Yes," he said in a thick German accent, "do you want to become one of my students?"

"Yes," I responded without hesitation.

A week later I returned to his studio, a simple room with the wooden cello case, two cellos, a viola de gamba (an early music instrument sometimes called a "cousin" of the cello), an upright piano, a tea kettle, a full-length mirror, a table, two wooden chairs, and a mattress on the floor, which the cellist used for naps between student appointments. His name was Heinrich Joachim, but I came to call him Mr. J.

"Tea or coffee?" he said when I came for my first lesson. And that became our routine. We would talk at that table over hot drinks for a few minutes and only then would we play cello. Mr. J wanted to know about my life and my ambitions before we even touched the instrument. I told him about those special Saturday morning walks with my dad on the way to synagogue, about how I lost my voice and how, in writing, I found another personal expression. "I don't even give music much thought anymore," I told him. "But when you opened your door and I saw you and I saw the cello, I thought this might be a way back for me."

Mr. J was warm and reassuring. "The cello," he said, "will give you back your voice."

When I told him about my concern about my age—I was twenty-six at the time—he laughed gently and told me not to worry. "There is something inside you we will have to bring out. But it will take work. Many years of work. I promise you, it will be worth it."

Mr. J was a great listener. It was harder for me to get him to open up about his life. He told me only bits and pieces. But over the years, and with the help of his children, I was able to assemble a realistic portrait of the man and his music.

HEINRICH JOACHIM WAS BORN in Berlin in 1910, the son of a Jewish doctor named Georg and a Catholic seamstress named Bertha. Heinrich was the third of seven children, all of whom played instruments from a very young age. Georg himself played the violin and organized musical evenings at home for his children and friends. Heinrich, who began piano at five, took up cello a year later. According to family lore, one day when he was eleven, Heinrich, dressed in a suit and tie with his hair slicked back with pomade, announced to the family that he was giving all his playthings to his younger brother

Gerhard. "From now on I am going to devote myself to the cello," he said in utmost seriousness. "For me, there is nothing else." A few years later, his parents sent him off to study with Adolf Steiner, one of the leading cellists of the day, and by the time Heinrich was nineteen, he became the principal cellist of a small chamber orchestra in Berlin that was an arm of the German Ministry of Culture. The year was 1929 and Hitler's rise to power had begun. By 1933, with Hitler firmly in control as chancellor, all members of the orchestra had to sign a loyalty oath to Hitler and the Nazi Party. Mr. J refused and lost his post.

Soon afterward, cello in hand, he boarded an ocean liner bound for Guatemala. He had no money and knew he would have to earn a living upon his arrival, so he spent the better part of the two weeks at sea learning Spanish. He was a quick study. By the time he reached Puerto Barrios, the main Guatemalan seaport on the Caribbean, he had serviceable Spanish.

Mr. J secured a job at the music conservatory in Guatemala City where he taught cello and music theory. He eventually became the head of the conservatory and made a name for himself as a chamber musician and orchestra soloist. In Guatemala, he ran into another German refugee, Ilonka Breitenbach, a singer five years his senior, whom he knew from the musical evenings in his home in Berlin. They married in Guatemala and had two children, Andrew and Dorothea.

Once again, however, Mr. J became the victim of a government decree. His job at the conservatory was a government post and, after World War II, Guatemala decided to purge foreigners from all government positions. He was without a job, and, by this time, his marriage was deteriorating. He divorced Ilonka and left her and the children behind in Guatemala to move to New York in search of work.

Before long, he set himself up in New York as a chamber musician and found a position as the principal cellist of the New York City Symphony Orchestra, which played at City Center under the leadership of a young conductor named Leonard Bernstein. The orchestra, which had been founded by Leopold Stokowski, was aimed at a younger classical music audience, offering more modern music and cheaper tickets than the New York Philharmonic. When the orchestra folded in 1948, Bernstein wrote Mr. J a letter of recommendation that said: "His tone is most pleasing, his musicianship sincere and sensitive, and his devotion to music unswerving."

Around the same time, Mr. J met a graceful young pianist named Renata Garve, like him a German refugee. They married and set up a house in Westchester County, just north of New York City. Mr. J and his new wife went to Guatemala to pick up Andrew, who was then eight years old. Ilonka and Dorothea moved to Germany to set up a new life there.

Mr. J and Renata had a son, Bruno, born in 1951 and named for the great German-born conductor Bruno Walter. A year later, the couple made their New York debut as a piano-cello duo at Town Hall. The review in the *Times* was a rave. "Mr. Joachim's cello sang with a warm, strong voice, tinted with the dark and rosy luster of the instrument itself," wrote the *Times* reviewer Carter Hermon. "The tone had body, but it was smooth and clear even in the lowest register and it was capable of light stage-whispers of attractive feathery quality."

At the time, Mr. J was a member of the cello section of the Philharmonic, where he stayed for nine years—under Stokowski, Dimitri Mitropoulos, and finally Bernstein—before leaving to become the principal cellist at the Balti-more Symphony under Peter Herman Adler in 1959. With his family rooted in New York's Westchester County,

Mr. J commuted to Baltimore for concerts. But things were not good at home. To hear Andrew tell it, Renata was not kind to her stepson.

"Stepmonster," he told me years later. He recalled being excluded from "family vacations" that involved Renata and Bruno but not him. They went off to Maine as a family while he was sent to summer camp. They went to Europe while he stayed with Renata's parents, where he remembers being barely tolerated if not ignored.

When he was ready for high school, Andrew boarded with a family in New York City and used their address to gain admission. He remembers never having enough money for food. His father lived by certain German aphorisms about money like *Sparsamkeit erhalt das haus* (Frugality keeps the house). There was actually virtue in hunger, his father would say, quoting another German proverb, *Hunger ist der beste koch* (Hunger is the best cook).

In 1962, tragedy struck. Renata was diagnosed with cancer and did not respond to treatment. She was forty-two when she died.

Mr. J, devastated by Renata's death, quit the Baltimore Symphony because he was needed at home to take care of Bruno, who was twelve. Andrew was already on his own, although he told me he was on his own emotionally years earlier.

Mr. J stopped concertizing and found work as a "section player" in various local orchestras and teaching music at the Manhattan School of Music and other conservatories. By the time I met him in 1976, he had married and divorced again (his third wife, Ursula Hirsch, was a former student of his) and was the father of a ten-year-old daughter, his fourth child, Angie.

"My father was a wonderful human being," Andrew said. "He was very sensitive, altruistic, and insightful. However, he was a terrible father, and had very few social skills, owing to his having devoted himself so exclusively to the cello at such a young age."

Andrew told me several cringe-worthy stories about his father. Unlike other fathers who wore fedoras in the 1960s, Mr. J wore a beret. Though he didn't like neckties, he wore them because it was the convention of the day, but they inevitably clashed with the colorful sport shirts he wore. His children hated to go shopping with him. "He would go into a discount store and inquire if the merchandise he was buying was of top quality," Andrew recalled. Then he would ask if he could get a further discount because he was a musician. When he would finally make a purchase, he complained about the plastic bag the merchandise was put in. "He would request a more colorful bag because, he said, it looked more 'gay,'" meaning festive. On top of it all, he spoke with a heavy German accent.

"To say the least, we were extremely embarrassed and annoyed," Andrew told me. "Heinrich was a uniquely strange man. Yes, he was a terrible father, but so out of touch that one could hardly hold that against him."

A TERRIBLE FATHER, PERHAPS; but a superb teacher. He made the cello come alive for me. More than anyone I've met, Mr. J saw the cello in human terms.

He'd take the cello and slowly run his hands down it from top to bottom. *Here, at the top, is the head. It even has ears, these pegs that you tweak when it sings out of tune. The head is connected to the long slender neck, which ends in the sloping shoulders. It has a back and, when I turn it over, a belly, both of them slightly arched. Overall, it has the feel of a rather womanly body, with a slim waist in between the curves. And, finally, it stands on a single leg, which we call the end pin.*

Sometimes when I arrived at his studio for a lesson, he'd be playing his viola da gamba and he'd say sheepishly, *The cello is my wife, but the gamba is my mistress!*

When I first took hold of the cello, he told me not simply to hold it but to fully embrace it *like you would hug a beautiful woman*. I put my arms around the neck and my legs around the body of the instrument. *Now play,* he said, instructing me to run the bow over the strings. *Don't just listen to the sound. Feel the sound. Feel the vibrations, not only in your hands but up your thighs and on your chest. Feel the sound.*

The cello is something of an enigma, he taught me. It has the body of a woman, with an ample curved bottom, a narrow waist, and a full curved top. And the cello has what musicians call f-holes —orifices shaped like two bold italic *f*s—which some musicians liken to the mouth, ears, and eyes of a woman. And, yet, for all these feminine attributes, the cello has a man's voice. Its tonal range most approximates that of a man, sounding at times like the bass singer in a barbershop quartet and at other times like the quartet's male alto.

But then it has something that is both male and female. *It has a soul.*

For Mr. J, the soul of the cello was the sound post, that small dowel of wood that sits inside the cello and transfers the sound from the top panel of the instrument to the back panel and beyond. *You can't see it, but believe me, it is there,*

inside, set right under the bridge of the cello. If the sound post
falls, your cello sounds weak, hollow, and thin, but with the
sound post in place, it has not just sound but soul.

Mr. J's anthropomorphic notions had a great impact
on me. Playing the cello was not simply a mechanical act
but an engagement with another body and another soul.
It meant commitment, respect, loyalty, devotion, even
love.

The first order of business was to buy an instrument
of my own. Adult full-sized cellos are expensive, with a
starting price of a thousand dollars for anything decent.
From there the sky's the limit, and some Stradivaris and
Guarneris are worth millions of dollars. Adults who take
up the cello are advised to rent first. All too often, adults
fall out of love with the instrument or simply feel it is too
hard to master. (The parents of children are also advised
to rent, not only because the child might stop playing, but
because youth cellos come in different sizes and as soon as
you buy a quarter- or half-size cello for your child, he or
she may outgrow it.)

But I didn't want to rent. After meeting Mr. J, I knew
that I was in this for life. "I'm ready to buy," I told Mr. J
after our first lesson. He offered to go shopping with me
but stopped and then thought a moment and added: "I

might just have something at home that will work for you. It doesn't look like much but it has a sweet sound."

When I returned the next week, Mr. J took out a cello that was dark red in color. "This is 'Bill,' named for my friend Bill Robson, who gave it to me as a gift. Don't be alarmed by all the nicks and cracks—or by the bullet hole in the front. I'm not sure how that got there, but it was nicely mended."

I wondered who was shooting at Bill. The bullet hole, patched with a peg of wood, was right over where Bill's heart might have been. "Bill" was a student cello, one built in the 1920s in France. Mr. J said he would sell it to me for five hundred dollars.

I was about to agree, but then he stopped me and said, "You must hear it first." Of course, I thought. I was like the first-time car buyer who was ready to buy the car on the lot and without a test-drive, always a big mistake. Mr. J tuned the instrument and played each of the strings with the bow, the series simply called open strings. "A, D, G, C," the notes rang out. In his hands, this student cello had a warm and generous sound. When I took it in my hands, it didn't sound nearly as good. It sounded scratchy and uneven.

You need a ninety-degree angle. That's ninety degrees where the bow meets the string and you must maintain it

as you move the bow down and as you move the bow up.
I wasn't getting it and Mr. J, ever patient, corrected me
again and again and again. He finally had me stand up and
move my chair in front of the full-length mirror he kept
in his studio. *Now watch your bow. Watch your bow. Keep
watching it until the ninety-degree angle becomes second nature.* Little did I know that this would take years and years
of practice. It would be years, in fact, before I could even
approximate the sound Mr. J got out of that cello, even
on open strings. *In making music, the cello counts,* Mr. J
explained, *but the cellist counts even more.*

Mr. J and I discussed sound quality, what musicians call
timbre. The particular sound of a particular instrument is
its timbre, also known as tone color. It is what makes one
musical sound different from another even when they have
the same pitch and volume. For example, an A played on
a cello will sound different from an A played on a gamba
and an A played on a piano.

Mr. J demonstrated by playing all three A's on the instruments that surrounded him in his studio. *The piano
A, the cello A, the gamba A, they are all the same note but
they have a different timbre. And even an A on your cello
sounds different than an A on mine.* Again, he paused and
demonstrated.

It's like men and women talking. You can tell which is the man and which is the woman. That is because of timbre. But more than that. Just like you can tell one man from another and one woman from another, you can tell one cello from another and one cellist from another. Timbre makes the difference.

LOVE AND MARRIAGE

I took weekly lessons with Mr. J for seven years, and with each lesson I found more of my rhythm, melody, harmony, and timbre.

At the same time, I was advancing in my reporting career, moving from a suburban reporter to a city reporter specializing in education, politics, transportation, and eventually religion. I would often have to cancel lessons because of deadlines and travel, but Mr. J was understanding. He knew my job came first. If anything, I was the one who felt bereft when I didn't have a lesson. I needed some harmony in my life.

In those special moments before each formal lesson began, I told Mr. J about my new beats and my growing body of articles. He wasn't a regular *Times* reader and he asked me to bring my articles to our lessons so he could see what I was up to. I would clip them out and show them off like so many baby pictures. I took pride in my work but I wanted more. I was quickly moving through my early thirties and I wanted my own family—with real baby pictures.

One week I told Mr. J that I was dating a girl and thinking of marriage. "I must meet her," he said. Shira had not yet met my father, although I had introduced her to my mother. I wasn't keeping Shira from my dad; it was just that he never asked. Mr. J asked. I brought Shira to the next lesson and he, like me, was smitten. Shira, eleven years my junior, is gorgeous with an equally high-wattage personality. Was then; is now. But what captivated me most, from the start, was her voice.

I am a sucker for a beautiful voice. My mother, Judith, couldn't sing but, oh, could she talk. There was energy, melody, rhythm, harmony, grace, and a range of expression— from surprise to joy to concern to sadness—that no instrument could duplicate. My mother, born in Brooklyn, was the eldest of four girls in her family. She had an older brother, but no one held a candle to her oratorical abilities. She was articulate and commanding. She trained to be a teacher at Brooklyn College and then got an advanced degree in library science from Columbia. She devoured books like a hungry man devours food. She read everything and seemed to remember everything, not just the stories, but the words and expressions used to tell the stories. And she made these words and stories her own. Her voice was the sound track of my childhood.

I first heard Shira's voice on the phone. She, a rabbi's daughter, was just out of college and was calling, on the recommendation of a "mutual friend," with questions about a career in journalism. In observant Jewish circles, I was the go-to person to talk about journalism. But I barely listened to Shira's questions. I was taken by the voice. With some callers, a few minutes on the phone would suffice, but Shira left me hankering for more. I always suspected that our "mutual friend" knew I would fall in love. Shira and I met a short while later for breakfast and, within a few months, we were engaged.

"Beautiful voice," Mr. J said approvingly.

Shira and I married in 1983, in the backyard of the Westport, Connecticut, home that my mother shared with her second husband. Mr. J came and brought along his cello. As Shira and I stood under the marital canopy, he played "Air on the G String" by Bach and "The Swan" by Saint-Saëns.

Our first child, Adam, came within our first year of marriage. To honor Mr. J, we gave Adam the middle name of Joachim. I felt closer than ever to Mr. J and even kept up sessions with him until Adam was about a year old, but I soon found that the demands of job and family were overwhelming; I simply had no time for music lessons, let alone practicing. It was a wrenching decision, but I stopped my regular lessons and put the cello away. I was thirty-five years old and the time had come to concentrate on other things. But I stayed in touch with Mr. J—after all, he had become something of a father to me—and I always knew I would return to music one day. My cello was in a closet but it was not forgotten, just waiting for the right moment.

Four years later Shira and I had a daughter and named her Emma. We had no relative or music teacher named Emma, but I always had wanted to be related to the great anarchist-feminist Emma Goldman and, now, finally, I was. When Emma was turning five years old, I gave up my reporting job at the *New York Times* and took a faculty position at Columbia University's Graduate School of Journalism. And then, fresh in my new life as a professor, we had a third child, Judah, named for my mother, who had died just a few weeks before his birth.

ALL OF OUR CHILDREN proved to be musical, Adam gravitating toward the piano and Emma blessed with a lovely singing voice. But it was Judah who was the first to show any interest in the cello. One day when he was six, I took my cello out of the closet, liberated it from its dusty wooden case, tuned it up, and played for him. "This is Bill," I told him, and, using Mr. J's cosmology, showed him Bill's head, ears, neck, body, and single leg. "Where's the other one?" Judah asked. I told him that Bill was from France and was injured in the French Revolution. "Come closer," I said. "Look, he even has a bullet wound in his chest." Judah looked at the patched-up hole in wonder.

It had been decades since I had played with Mr. J and I didn't really remember any songs but still knew how to tune the instrument, and I could nicely manage open strings. "A, D, G, C," I sang along.

Then I showed Judah how I could play a song out of these four notes. It is a little melody that Mr. J taught me called "Sheila's Open String Waltz." It goes DDD, AAA, DDGD, AAAD. First I plucked the strings then I bowed them, swaying with a dance-like rhythm. Then I showed him a little open string march called "A Toy Regimen."

Judah's eyes widened and he tried to hold the cello and imitate my motions. It was, of course, a full-size adult cello and Judah could not get his arms around it. But I had him put his hand on mine as I bowed. "It's vibrating, Daddy!" he exclaimed. Then I told him to put his ear directly on the wooden back so he could hear the soul of the cello. "That tickles," he said and laughed.

"Judah, do you know that they make cellos for children your size?"

I let the thought sink in.

"I know a place where we can get one and maybe we can find a teacher for you so you can play cello, too."

"Yes," Judah said. "Let's go."

I explained that it would still be a few days before I could arrange everything but that we would do it soon.

I was about to put the instrument back in its wooden case when I told Judah to say "good-bye" to the cello for now. He then did something extraordinary. He leaned over and kissed the cello good-night.

PART THREE

FATHERS AND SONS

AND ORCHESTRAS

> Music is the divine way to tell
> beautiful, poetic things to the heart.
> —PABLO CASALS

In Judaism there is the concept of the *ba'al teshuva,* one who "returns" to the faith. Curiously, such people—we might call them Jewish late starters—are seen as *returning* to the faith even if they never were observant to begin with. The idea is that observance is the "natural state" of a Jew and that, as we take steps toward tradition, we are in a very real sense going back to our essence.

This notion of return centers on one of my favorite Jewish myths, the one about the angel Gabriel, who is said to visit every Jewish child in the womb and teach him, or her, all of Torah—Torah being used here in the broadest sense: Jewish lore, law, and wisdom. It is a wonderful image to contemplate, especially since Gabriel is said to carry a lantern to light his way in the darkness of the womb.

However, right before the baby goes out into the world,

Gabriel blows out the light and gently strikes the child over the mouth (hence the indentation between the upper lip and nose)—and all the learning is forgotten. Life, this story teaches, is about reclaiming what we already know.

In learning music—and in sharing it with my children—I sometimes have the sense that I am recapturing something intrinsic to me rather than learning something alien and new. This was especially true in the lessons taught by Mr. J. When he reminded me that *the music is in you,* I wondered if Gabriel also gave me music lessons in the womb alongside the lessons of Torah. Perhaps learning cello as a late starter was not about learning it anew but about recapturing what was already part of me.

AS WITH TORAH, I believed that there was a right way and wrong way to do music. I had certain orthodoxies about classical music, ideas influenced in no small measure by Mr. J.

First, *there is no higher art form*. Paintings are nice, architecture can be inspiring, mathematics has its moments, engineering is a marvel, but classical music is the pinnacle of creation. Jazz, rock, and folk have their place, but classical music is the God music and the God of all art forms.

Second, *classical music was written for one purpose: to be listened to.* All other music can be interrupted. You can talk at a jazz club; go ahead, bob your head and tap your foot. You can sing along with the folksingers at the hootenanny; Pete Seeger will even prompt the next verse. You've got to get on your feet, dance, jump into a mosh pit, or wave a match (or your lighted cell phone) at a rock concert. But you must sit still at the symphony. And listen. There is no such thing as incidental music. Music is the main course.

With obvious joy, Mr. J would quote G. K. Chesterton, the English literary and social critic, who said: "Music with dinner is an insult both to the cook and the violinist."

Third, *classical music is telling us something important.* It demands active listening and, if you indeed listen, you will experience powerful feelings that stimulate the imagination and touch the soul. It speaks to us, not just in some metaphorical sense, but in real, actual language. It is, simply put, more powerful than words.

Fourth, recordings are okay, but *nothing equals the experience of hearing music live, in a concert hall, where you can connect with the musicians and the mind and soul can focus.*

Fifth, *this is the music you never tire of.* You learn something from every encounter with classical music. I cannot listen to the same rock song over and over again. Being stuck in a car with a "classic rock" or "Top 40" radio station is my worst nightmare. I do not want music of the seventies or eighties or nineties, as some popular radio stations advertise. I want the music of the seventeen hundreds and eighteen hundreds and early nineteen hundreds. Over and over and over again.

All these orthodoxies have been debunked again and again. Some say that adherence to them has led to a serious decline in the classical music audience. A recent survey by the League of American Orchestras indicated that the number of people who attend classical music concerts has been declining for almost three decades, from 13 percent to just over 9 percent. That means that fewer than one in ten American adults has attended a classical music concert in the last year.

On the other hand, the declines are across the board, in all age ranges, and represent a drop in all experiences that demand that a person venture out and travel to a venue, take a seat, and watch or listen. This is true of movies, plays, and jazz and rock concerts. Sporting events have suffered the most, with a 36 percent drop in the last thirty years.

At the same time, the American League of Orchestras' survey notes, more people are listening to classical music than ever before. The growth is all digital; that is, online or on the radio. People are downloading classical music they love or exploring it on websites like Pandora or Spotify. Meanwhile, the sale of classical music, either on CDs or online, continues to tumble.

To deal with the crisis in classical music, orchestras are coming up with new marketing techniques and reviving old ones. They are offering more diverse concerts, with classical and show tunes alongside jazz, and are moving concerts out of doors to bandstands and public parks where people come with blankets and picnic baskets and either listen or ignore the music. People talk, arrive late, leave early, eat, and even applaud between movements.

It's a tactic that seems to be working but is something of a compromise. For me, nothing equals sitting in a proper concert hall and listening to great music. To play cello in such a venue is my ultimate musical aspiration.

DOWNTOWN SYMPHONY

My initial success with LSO emboldened me to stretch more and explore the Downtown Symphony, an amateur adult orchestra that has been in existence for more than twenty-five years at the Borough of Manhattan

Community College in Lower Manhattan. The orchestra gives four public concerts every year including an annual *Messiah* sing-in at Christmastime. After I heard about the Downtown Symphony from Eve and Mary at my first Late Starters rehearsal, I checked out its website. There, I saw these dreaded words, which Mary had already warned me about:

"Admission to the orchestra is by audition."

I read on. In this audition, I would need to "play scales," "sight-read," and "play two contrasting pieces" of music. I knew numerous scales and I had at least two simple pieces in my repertoire (though I wasn't sure if they were contrasting enough), but sight-reading? For me, that's like seeing a mathematical formula and recognizing all the numbers and symbols without having a clue of how to solve it. It looks familiar but what does it all mean? I knew I wasn't ready for this audition, but Mary's words kept ringing in my ears:

"You may not live long enough to be 'good enough.'"

I screwed up my courage and called Doug Anderson, the Downtown Symphony conductor, and scheduled an audition for late one winter night after work. Doug was warm and friendly when I met him in his crowded office at the college, where he is a professor of music. I told him that I had been playing on and off for a long, long time but that I still considered myself something of a beginner. "Most everyone who comes is like you," Doug said. He told me that only a handful of the fifty players in the orchestra were music students or faculty members; most were amateur musicians who ranged in age from eighteen to eighty. He cleared away some books and papers in his office and I set out my cello. I told him I was a little rusty and a little nervous about the audition. He sought to calm me down. "Listen, Ari. We are a learning orchestra, not a terrorist organization . . . like some other orchestras. We're here to have fun."

I laughed nervously and threw myself into my music. I made it through the scales okay and the two short pieces that I had prepared. I thought I noted a trace of a sympathetic smile on his face, but then I was playing pieces from my son's Suzuki cello book. "Nice," he said slowly, which was a sure sign that he wasn't convinced. Doug then handed me a page of sheet music by the French composer Georges Bizet. I knew that Bizet wrote the opera *Carmen,* but this was not a trivia test. It was an audition and I was supposed to play—by sight—music that I had never seen or heard before.

I put the Bizet on my music stand, studied it for a few

seconds, smiled wanly, and said, "Honestly, I don't know where to begin."

What's the key signature? I suddenly heard Mr. J asking. *That's where our understanding of the music begins.* The key signature consists of one or more notes arranged on the five staff lines at the very top of a piece of sheet music. *Reading music,* I heard Mr. J say, *is like reading English or German or Chinese or any other language. The key signature, in effect, tells you what language you are in. Think of it this way: the key signature tells you the language, the notes are words, the measures are sentences, the lines are phrases, and the cadences are periods. Now read!*

I took a closer look at the Bizet. I saw a C# and an F#. I knew that meant that our "language" was the key of D. Then, haltingly, I played the first note, and the second and the third and soon a musical story began to emerge. I thought I was doing well and eagerly looked to Doug for an assessment.

"Let me be honest with you," Doug began. "I'd love to have you in the orchestra. You seem dedicated and interested in learning. You've got the right attitude. But this might be frustrating for you. At the beginning you'll be playing about 10 percent of the music I hand out. By the time the concert comes, you'll probably be up to 50 percent. Next year, even more. But it's going to be tough at first. If you don't think it will be too frustrating for you, you're in."

"I'm in?" I said almost disbelieving what I had just heard. I actually passed the audition? Is that possible? Whoopeee! I tried to remain cool. "Okay," I said with a smile. "I'll give it a shot."

A week later I showed up for my first rehearsal. I had none of the jitters that accompanied my first Late Starters rehearsal. I auditioned. I was accepted. I was ready. The Downtown Symphony met in a proper soundproofed music room at the community college, not at all like the makeshift rehearsal space of the LSO. And unlike LSO, which was all strings, this orchestra included oboes, clarinets, flutes, and horns. It even had a percussion section, complete with various drums, cymbals, and a gong. There were about fifty of us in all, including my friends Eve and Mary from LSO. I had to pinch myself. I felt like Pinocchio in Geppetto's toy shop. I was a real boy in a real orchestra!

The rehearsal began. We were playing passages from Tchaikovsky's "1812 Overture," a piece I've always loved. What a full, rich sound! It was thrilling to be sitting in the middle of all that thunder and excitement. I surprised myself by being able to keep up with more than 10 percent of the score. I was with them 20 or even 30 percent of the time, but then I already knew the music, just from hearing it so many times. Knowing the melodies always makes them easier to play.

During the break I spoke to some of the other musicians and was gratified to learn that I was not the only one who was lost. "Do you figure it out by the time of the concert?" I asked a young man who played the double bass.

"Well, most of it," he answered.

"Isn't there a lot of pressure on you to get it right?"

"No," another musician, a violinist, chimed in. "At the concert, Doug brings in some pros who lead the way."

"You mean he brings in ringers?"

"Well, we call them subs."

"Who are they substituting for?"

"The rest of us."

It sounded like a good thing. You bring in some real good players and that brings up everyone's game. I asked if any of the "ringers" were at the rehearsal that night.

"They never come to rehearsals," my new friend the double bassist told me. "They're pros. They just show up the night of the concert. Now don't worry. We have backup."

After the break, I went back to playing with greater confidence. Performing with a safety net sounded perfect.

MILT

On the subway going home that night I ran into an older man bundled in a winter coat and carrying a violin case. "Excuse me," I said, "weren't you at the Downtown Symphony tonight?"

He was indeed and we introduced ourselves and spoke as we rode uptown. His name was Milt, a retired physician in his eighties, and his story was not atypical of late starters. Milt took up the violin as a young boy in New Jersey and played through high school and into college. "When I was nineteen, I was admitted to medical school and I put my violin away and never touched it again for fifty years," he said. Medicine became his life. He finished medical school and opened what he described as a thriving family practice in his home state.

He worked out of his home office, later out of a private doctor's office, and even later out of a clinic. He told me that he treated several generations in some families. "Grandparents, parents, children. They just kept coming. And then one day, I closed my practice. I went home, found my old violin in the attic and picked it up again," he said. "And I haven't put it down since."

Milt said he had "to learn it all over again," but that it came back, slowly, step by step. "Music is my life now. After retirement, there is nothing else."

He and his wife sold their New Jersey home and moved to the Upper West Side of Manhattan in part because they wanted to be near Lincoln Center for the Performing Arts. One of their favorite activities is attending the Philharmonic's "open rehearsals," where, for less than twenty dollars, you can hear great music and see how it is shaped by the conductor and the musicians. The open rehearsals begin at 9:45 in the morning. "You get to go for a fraction of the price of what people pay to go to the same concert in the evening," Milt said. "And I love to watch how the sausage is made."

I had not heard of the Philharmonic's open rehearsals in decades and was surprised that they still existed. I remember going a few times in college. I called Richard Wandel, an archivist for the Philharmonic, who told me that these musical sessions were as old as the orchestra itself, which is pretty old since the New York Philharmonic, the oldest standing orchestra in the United States, played its first season well before the Civil War. Open rehearsals began in 1842 under the very first musical director, Ureli Corelli Hill. The sessions were at first intended to give the orchestra a chance to prepare before a live audience without the pressure of a formal performance. With time, they also became a way to involve people who otherwise might not attend the more expensive official programs.

For Milt, the open rehearsals are also a way to involve his wife, who is not a musician. Milt inspired me to check them out as well. On the winter morning I attended, the audience was made up of mostly older, retired folks. Who else can take off a morning for music, except perhaps for a professor, like me, or some students? The audience filled only about half the seats in the orchestra and the balconies were pretty much empty. I had paid $18 for my seat, a seat that would cost $115 if I had decided to go to the same program that evening.

The members of the Philharmonic, who play their concerts in formal wear, came straggling in as though they had just climbed out of bed, casually dressed in jeans, T-shirts, and sneakers. I was thinking that my fellow LSO musicians come better dressed. There wasn't a tie or jacket on stage. I was trying to imagine Mr. J trundling onto the stage with his cello for an open rehearsal when he was in the Philharmonic in the 1950s. Given his penchant for eccentric dress, he would have shown up in a paisley shirt and plaid pants. And he would have fit right in.

Works by Mozart, Mahler, and a contemporary composer named Thomas Adès were on the program. No one on stage budged when Alan Gilbert, the Philharmonic's youthful music director, appeared—at a proper performance all the musicians would stand—but the audience gave Gilbert a warm round of applause. Gilbert took a short bow and then acted as if we in the audience weren't there. He stopped the orchestra when he felt it necessary and had them repeat passages that he was unhappy with. Sometimes he'd sing a few measures out loud to demonstrate what he was looking for. Gilbert, who took over the orchestra in 2009 at the age of forty-two, seemed decidedly at home. But that was no wonder since both his mother and father had careers as violinists with the Philharmonic. (His father, Michael Gilbert, retired in 2001, and his mother, Yoko Takebe, continues to perform with the orchestra.)

I was hoping to connect with Milt and his wife at the open rehearsal that morning, but we didn't manage to meet. Aside from the mornings at Lincoln Center, Milt told me that he practices his violin every day and takes a lesson once a week with his teacher. He plays with the

Downtown Symphony one night and with a chamber music group for seniors at the Mannes College one morning a week. "Truth is, I'm not all that good," he lamented that night we met on the train. "I wish I knew what I forgot. My fingers aren't that quick. But everyone tolerates me. And I love it."

When we reached his stop near Lincoln Center, he said, "Hope I see you again next week, Ari. Good luck with the music."

As it turned out, the Downtown Symphony was not the right fit for me. It met on Tuesday nights, which meant I was out of commission on the home front. That wasn't really fair to Shira, whose public relations business, which she ran alone, seemed to take more and more of her time, often into the evenings. There were dinners to prepare and Judah's homework—and cello playing—to supervise. But it was more than just a question of timing. The music was a real leap for me. It was well beyond what we were playing at LSO, where we were more likely to tackle four-part arrangements of chamber music than full-blown symphonies. I felt foolish after begging Doug for a place at the Downtown Symphony, but ultimately he was right. It wasn't for me. I decided to focus on my own playing and on LSO.

SUZUKI

After Judah gave the cello a kiss on the night I first showed it to him, I started asking around about cello teachers. I was advised not to look for a teacher, but for a method: Suzuki.

Suzuki is an extraordinary system of musical education for youngsters. It is based on the teachings of Shinichi Suzuki, a Japanese educator and violinist who died at the age of ninety-nine in 1998. Suzuki was committed to the idea that a child can learn music the same way that he or she learns language: through immersion, encouragement, repetition, and small steps. It is sometimes called the "mom-centric" method of music education because of the heavy parental involvement necessary to make it work, but dads are also welcome. From the time Judah turned six, I took him each week to a program near Lincoln Center.

Judah began with an eighth-size cello, an instrument not much bigger than a violin. But instead of holding it under his chin, as a violinist would, Judah's teacher taught him how to pull out the end pin and place the cello between his legs. Much to my delight, he took to it. The Suzuki method gently introduces the instrument to the child. First the child learns by ear and only later does he or she learn musical notation. The child begins with something familiar—the letters of the alphabet—rather than notes on a musical staff. An early Suzuki piece might look like this: DDAABBA GGFFEED. AABBCCA BBAACCA. That's "Twinkle, Twinkle, Little Star."

Judah's first teacher, a Korean cellist named Sujin, was warm and funny and rewarded him at the end of each lesson with animal stickers on his practice book. She managed to turn everything into a game. Judah played "Twinkle" to death. Who knew there were so many variations, each one with its own rhythm and style but all unmistakably "Twinkle"? She named each one. There was "Ice Cream Twinkle" and "Choo-Choo Twinkle" and "Cha-Cha Twinkle." After mastering the "Twinkle" repertoire, Judah graduated to songs like "Go Tell Aunt Rhody," "French Folk Song," "The Happy Farmer," and even a simple minuet or two by Bach.

I happily sat through lessons and practiced each night with Judah. He was in first grade when we began and was just getting into the rhythm of nightly homework. Cello practice became part of his nightly routine—and mine. Just ten minutes in the beginning, but then fifteen and even twenty as he moved up through the grades. It was never onerous; always fun. Playing music became as natural as dinner, homework, and bedtime.

The Suzuki books start easy but quickly accelerate to more challenging material. By the end of Book 1, which is mostly made up of familiar folk songs, the young cellist is playing a minuet from a manuscript known as the *Notebook for Anna Magdalena Bach,* presented by the composer to his second wife. The notebooks provide a glimpse into the domestic music of the eighteenth century, a time when, if you wanted music in your life, you had to create it. It was exhilarating to know that the same music being played in Bach's house was being played in ours.

By the second Suzuki book, children have left folk songs and family dances behind and are playing Mozart, Handel, and Schumann. Successive books become more demanding in terms of bowing, speed, and position. By Book 4, the young cellist gets to play selections from the Bach suites that Pablo Casals made famous. From there, the repertoire is vast and accessible. Students are soon playing Beethoven, Dvořák, Tchaikovsky, and Boccherini. In our house, we would make a party with cupcakes and ice cream when Judah finished one of the Suzuki books and moved on to the next.

When Judah started lessons, I called Mr. J to tell him that there was a new cellist in the family. Mr. J had just turned ninety and I checked in with him every few weeks just to say hello. He was overjoyed to hear about Judah. "How wonderful," he said. "My musical son has a musical son." I promised to drive up one day to show him the wonder of Judah playing but I never managed to. One day, a year or so later, I got a call from Andrew that Mr. J had had a massive stroke. Andrew gave me the name of the hospital where he was being cared for in Westchester and I drove there the next day. He told me to prepare myself for a sad sight.

When I approached Mr. J's room, I first spotted his beautiful mane of hair, as white and luxuriant as ever. But beneath that hair, I saw a face contorted as if in permanent pain. Hands that once mastered the cello repertoire—and flirted with the gamba—were gnarled and clenched. Mr. J's eyes were open but it was clear that he did not see, not me, not anything. I sat vigil for the afternoon with Andrew and Angie and Angie's mother, Ursula. A few weeks later he was gone.

In the years after Mr. J's death, several new cello teachers came into my life, some for Judah and others for me, and one for both of us. But even with Mr. J gone, I still heard his voice, sometimes in my head, at other times in my dreams, and at still other times in the music of the cello.

JUDAH AND I HAD a routine on Tuesday nights. He'd come home from school, have a snack, and then we took the subway from our apartment at Columbia to his lesson on West Sixty-seventh Street. During his third year of Suzuki, though, I had the feeling that Judah was running in place. He was ready for the next level but I wasn't sure what that was. I began to ask around for a new cello teacher.

Early one morning while on an errand in my neighborhood, I turned the corner onto Broadway and found myself walking alongside a young woman with a cello on her back. She had curly blond hair and a happy bounce in her step.

I didn't want to come across as a weirdo but I had to ask. "Excuse me. Hello? Can I ask you a question?" The woman turned and looked at me suspiciously. "I'm sorry to bother you but do you know a good cello teacher for a nine-year-old boy?" She seemed more than a bit wary of me and of my question. "It's for my son. He's nine," I repeated. She stopped, seemed to size me up, and, I suppose, realized that I was sincere and not just giving her a line. I handed her my business card. She saw that I was a Columbia professor and then finally spoke.

"I teach," she said brightly. "Perhaps we can work something out."

Shira, too, was skeptical at first when I told her about how I found the new cello teacher. "So let me get this straight," she began. "You picked up a chick on the street because she happened to be wearing a cello? Are there no male cellists in Manhattan? Have you been interviewing all of them, too?" I didn't blame Shira for her caution but I convinced her that this was worth at least one lesson. Shira was sure to be home on the first day the new teacher arrived. Two minutes into the lesson, Shira was won over by this young woman, whose name was Laura. Most important, Judah took an instant liking to her.

Laura was in a joint undergraduate music program between Columbia and Juilliard but she was as much a cheerleader as a teacher. She came to our apartment on Sunday mornings, worked on Judah's technique, scales, and music—and inevitably took to her feet and gave him standing ovations for his work, which improved week to week at a rate that we had not seen before. Indeed, this was the next step that he needed.

Judah was already in his fourth year of cello lessons and had graduated from an eighth-size cello to a quarter-size to a half-size instrument. In the beginning I sat in on every lesson. I needed to know what Judah was learning so I could be sure he'd practice what he needed to learn. Judah and Laura sat in our living room on facing straight-backed chairs, their cellos between them. Laura would demonstrate a technique, a note, or a passage, and Judah would take what he saw and heard and make it his own. I would sit on the couch off to the side and literally feel the good vibrations. Like few other instruments, the cello resonates through the wood and the furniture and warms the body. I loved just sitting there.

With time I became superfluous. I marveled at the bond that was developing between the teacher and the student. It often reminded me of my relationship with Mr. J. "My dear cello-son Ari," he wrote to me a year before his death. The salutation came in a note he wrote to me about religion, a topic we often discussed. We had very different approaches to religion. Ritual practice was and is a very important part of my life but not his. In this letter he tried to bridge the gap between us. *Through the toil and studies of our instrument,* he wrote, *we were searching, I think for a "musical religion." Consider, for example, your Bach Prelude. Behind the simple black dots, which he wrote more than three hundred years ago, we endeavored to find and re-live the miracle of his spiritual and emotional creation.*

Judah's relationship with his teacher Laura was perhaps less philosophical but equally spiritual and emotional.

Judah was easy to fall in love with. He is our youngest, separated from his brother by eleven years and his sister by seven years. He relished his junior status in the family, and he was far more compliant than his siblings were at his age. Until he was a teenager, we never got an argument out of him. He listened. He also looked like the baby with his chubby build, curly dirty blond hair, and chipmunk cheeks. While other preteens couldn't wait to grow up, Judah savored his babydom. He liked the cartoon character Pajama Sam and he was an avid collector of Yu-Gi-Oh! cards. He even favored plastic dishes and tiny silverware when he ate.

I stopped sitting in on the lessons, but I never stopped listening to the music. My favorite moments were when Judah and Laura would play duets, simple pieces like the chorus from *Judas Maccabaeus* by Handel or the theme from "Witches' Dance" by Paganini. But even when Laura played along, the focus was on Judah. She'd put down her cello and give him a standing ovation.

Laura grew up playing the Suzuki method and was trained to teach it. As she was well connected in the Suzuki world, she recommended that we check out the summer Suzuki program in Hartford, Connecticut. We signed up, packed the car with Judah's half-size cello, and headed for Hartford, which, as it happens, is the city of my birth. Hartford has all sorts of associations for me. Although I moved away from Hartford when my parents divorced, I kept coming back throughout my childhood to spend weekends with my dad, who remained there for most of his life.

Suzuki camp is just a week long and a parent or other responsible adult is expected to be on hand to supervise. Judah went for four summers and, on our trips to Hartford, I showed Judah the sites: the hospital I was born in, my childhood home, the house where my grandparents lived, and even the Mark Twain House, Hartford's national landmark. But perhaps the place that made the greatest impression on him was the Crown Market, the kosher supermarket where we bought deli sandwiches practically every night after Suzuki camp.

On one trip, I even gave Judah a tour of the synagogues of Hartford, the one we went to (Orthodox) and, of course, the one my family would never step into (the

Conservative one). Judah and I caught a service one summer afternoon at the Orthodox Young Israel of West Hartford. A man a few years younger than me approached and asked, "Are you Marvin's son?" When I said yes, he warmly embraced me. "I thought that was you," he said. "We met several years ago at your father's apartment in Jerusalem. I was visiting Israel with my family and we shared a meal with you at his apartment."

The man's name was Stan and I had only the vaguest memory of meeting him in Israel. My father, who worked in real estate, had retired with his second wife to Jerusalem at the age of seventy. He lived out his remaining years there and died peacefully in Jerusalem at the age of seventy-seven.

"Your dad played a very important role in my life," Stan was saying. He told me how, as a boy of fourteen, he became attracted to greater Jewish observance and began to go to synagogue, often alone. My father, too, was sitting alone and soon they struck up a friendship. "We used to sit together every Shabbos," Stan said. "He became my mentor and advisor." Over the years, Stan became more involved Jewishly and aspired to go to Yeshiva University, which was the school of the men of my family (both my father and I went there, as did numerous uncles, both on my mother's side and on my father's side). My father saw Stan through the admissions process to Yeshiva and even secured financial aid for his first year of college, when Stan's parents balked at paying. Later, my father helped him and his wife purchase their first house in Hartford. "He held our hands throughout the process, guiding us and giving us confidence with every step," Stan said.

I had mixed emotions about all this. On the one hand, I was proud that my father was such a strong mentor. On the other, I was envious. In my teens I was living in New York with my mother and often sat alone in synagogue. My dad was not very much involved with my college education and was certainly not there when I bought my first house (which turned out to be a big financial mistake).

I remembered how Andrew had told me that Mr. J was a "terrible father" and how that was corroborated by events such as his leaving his family behind in Guatemala and his tolerance of his second wife's poor treatment of Andrew. Yet I idolized Mr. J and considered him not just my teacher, but my "musical father."

Perhaps, I mused, that is the nature of fathers and sons. As fathers we do our best to encourage and nurture and support. It is, however, an impossible job and, inevitably, we come up short. There isn't a child without complaint. There isn't a father without regrets.

Often, we fathers find, there's someone who does it better: a teacher, a friend, a mentor. Maybe not everything better, but some things, perhaps just enough to highlight our inadequacies. I suppose fathers have to be thankful for that someone else. These thoughts were rattling around my head as I traveled through Hartford with Judah for those four summers. I was hoping to be both a father and a mentor to him and yet wondering how well I would succeed at either.

THE SUMMER SUZUKI PROGRAM is housed at the Hartt School at the University of Hartford. The first summer that we went, Judah was in something called pre-orchestra, in which children learned where to sit (cellos to the right, violins to the left), how to stand when the conductor enters (in unison), how to be recognized if you have a question (raise your bow), and how to applaud with a bow in your hand (by stomping your feet). Playing music with other children was a new experience for him. Suzuki has a great parent-teacher support system but this was our first exposure to a broader musical world for children. It is one thing to hear your child play "Cha-Cha Twinkle" but to hear fifty little kids play it! That's a community dedicated to making music.

Judah made friends and also discovered more teachers who made learning fun. By his second summer at the Suzuki camp, Judah left pre-orchestra behind and was in a real youth orchestra. The conductor was a delightful educator named Dominic, a small man with a prominent mustache, bushy eyebrows, and just the right touch with kids. "Who knows vibrato?" he asked. Vibrato is the musical effect that a string player achieves by pulsating the left hand to produce slight and rapid variations in pitch. Again, I think of Mr. J. Although he often spoke in transcendent terms about voice, body, and mind, when it came to vibrato, he was much more down to earth. *Vibrato comes from the hand. There is nothing magical here. This is a mechanical function of the hand. If it is hard, it is because we are not used to it, but the hand can be taught.*

Vibrato is a technique that takes some time to develop and separates the more advanced student from the beginner. In one lovely children's book that Judah and I read, *The Facts and Fictions of Minna Pratt* by Patricia MacLachlan, the main character, a technically excellent cellist, awaits the coming of her vibrato the way most girls await their first period. Vibrato means you've come of age.

As Dominic asked the question to the Suzuki group, a few of the young musicians raised their bows, signaling that they had crossed the divide and knew vibrato. Judah was not there yet. Dominic seemed to be separating the haves from the have-nots, and I felt a pang of sorrow for my son and wondered if he felt it, too. But then Dominic burst the bubble with this instruction: "Good. Do it. Vibrato doesn't do anything but it looks good!"

Judah laughed. Dominic smiled, raised his baton, and the music started. Well, it sounded like music but soon deteriorated into cacophony. Everything went awry, even the vibrato. The cellos were way ahead of the violins and no one was in tune. "Why are you racing ahead?" he asked the cellos. "Okay. Who started it? Who is the ringleader? There's always a ringleader. Raise your hand if you are the ringleader." No one did.

Dominic scowled. "Good. You already know the first orchestra rule. It goes like this: If you make a mistake and the conductor asks, 'Who was that?' say, 'It wasn't me!' Blame someone else."

I watched Judah to see if he was mortified or amused. He was laughing so hard he could hardly play.

Judah's "repertory class" was taught by Nancy, a tall and lanky woman with big hands who seemed born to play the cello. She towered over the little children in the room even when she sat down. Her cello seemed formidable. The children, with half-size and quarter-size instruments, sat in front of her. A group of parents, some with notebooks open, ringed the room. Nancy put everyone at ease by having the children bang out tunes on their cellos and strum them like guitars. She had them play certain pieces together and then sent the parents out of the room. "That's new for Suzuki," one mother commented as we filed out and stood in the hall. (Suzuki seemed to have a never-ending appetite for parent involvement.)

Thirty minutes later we were invited to return and, after we took our seats, the children treated us to a "concert" of songs that they learned in our absence. It was a way of moving both the kids and us parents toward musical independence.

Later, a cellist named Rick held a "master class" that was limited to four students. It took me awhile to understand his method. He began by zeroing in on one child, asking him or her to play the newest piece of music they were working on. He'd wrinkle his brow and then pick out one aspect of their technique—the way she was holding the bow, the way he was sitting, the way her thumb grasped the neck of the cello—and have them repeat the music. He'd make the slightest correction and then ask them to play again. "Good. Much better," he'd say.

There are so many moving parts when it comes to playing the cello. First there is the human body, starting with the ten fingers, all of which are engaged in some way with the instrument. The cellist's feet must be planted firmly on the ground, the butt on the chair sitting at a right angle to the back, the arm grasping the bow yet flexible enough to reach across the full range of four strings. Then, there is the cello itself with the four pegs that are used for tuning and the metal end pin on which the instrument pivots when played.

Rick felt that Judah's left shoulder was too high. "You're tensing up. No need to do that. Just drop your shoulder down," he said. He gave Judah a good way to remember to do this. "Before you begin, raise your shoulder to your ear and then drop it down. Raise it and drop it. Good, that's it. Now pick up your bow."

I watched Judah and saw that it was difficult for him to keep the shoulder low. He did his best but it kept rising.

Watching him, I felt a sympathetic pain. I rubbed my neck, silently hoping that he would master this so we'd both feel better.

It wasn't all technique. Rick soon turned his attention to the other young players in the room as if noticing for the first time that they were there. But the focus was still on Judah. "What did you think of Judah's playing?" he asked.

"It was bouncy," one girl said.

"Good shifting," said another.

"Judah was having a good time," a boy said.

Now, with the new round of correction, critique, and encouragement, the child would play the piece again. After fifteen minutes, Rick would gently move on to the next young cellist. And the process of music, correction, encouragement, and group critique would begin again.

Rick's questions to the group would vary as the week went on. "What food did Sarah's piece sound like?" he'd ask. "Like chocolate," said one child. "Like juicy red meat," said another.

"What color?" "Red." "Purple." "Green." "Snow!"

Time whisked by. Judah played cello a good five hours a day for five days straight and didn't complain, even when I reminded him during a break that we'd have to spend a few minutes practicing. In the evening, the children put down their instruments and the faculty made music. One night a teacher played a gypsy-like piece by Ravel that began on stage but soon had her dancing through the audience of children.

"What did that make you feel like?" she asked the children when she was done. By this time they were more than musicians; they were experienced critics who could express their feelings about the music. The answers were so sophisticated that they took my breath away.

"It made me feel like crying," said one little boy.

"No. It was happy," said another child.

"Well, kind of happy and sad, like flying. It's exciting but scary."

"I felt something different," said another. "It was like . . . like rolling down a hill so fast, you can't stop!"

MUSIC MOMS AND DADS

Suzuki camp introduced me to the musical equivalent of the Soccer Mom, that devoted and sometimes pushy parent who, the stereotype goes, spends most of her time in the family minivan ferrying her offspring to soccer games and arguing with the coach for preferential treatment for her kids. Instead of carrying extra sneakers, socks, shin guards, and jerseys, the Cello Mom will carry a small stool (little cellists need little chairs), rosin (a chemical mixture rubbed on the bow to increase friction), extra strings, and sheet music. Between sessions at Suzuki camp, legions of music moms and dads—and sometimes grandparents, aunts, and uncles—could be seen toting the musical paraphernalia. Every child had a chaperone.

Some parents were musicians but this was not about their own playing. If any parents brought instruments along to Suzuki camp they didn't show them in public. The only taste of music-making we parents experienced was the "group singing chorus" where parents and children were encouraged to do voice exercises and sing together. Judah and I went once to the group singing chorus but found it totally boring. We were already musically bonded so we decided to cut that class.

Parents were expected to attend all classes with their children, except for orchestra. While the kids were in orchestra, we parents were encouraged to come to special classes about how to be a good Suzuki parent. There were sessions on such topics as "How to Encourage Good Practicing Habits," "How to Create a Music-Friendly Home

Environment," and "What to Do When Johnny Wants to Quit."

We gathered in a classroom on an upper floor of the Hartt School while our musical prodigies were in the studios below. It was a diverse crowd, although older parents, almost all of them women, tended to predominate. There weren't too many young moms in their twenties with a brood of kids. This was more the domain of the privileged older parent with one or at most two children, kids whom they could dote on. And while this was a BlackBerry and cell-phone crowd, parents paid attention. They did not pull out their PDAs. They had invested in their child's musical education and recognized that it wouldn't happen without them.

What inspires such parental devotion?

I am not sure about other parents, but for me it was a combination of emotions: the pleasure of the music, of course, but also anger and sadness. Simply put, I wish someone had done this for me. When I was six and seven and eight why didn't anyone nurture my musical gifts? I sang in school plays and in the synagogue, and I never tired of listening to music and watching musicians make music, either on television or live. Why didn't someone put a violin or cello in my hands? Why didn't my parents take me to music lessons? Why didn't they present me with the challenges of musical notation and vibrato and the camaraderie of the orchestra?

Perhaps my parents were unable to give me these things because they were so consumed by their own hard times. They divorced but they had no game plan after that. Neither of them could handle three young boys alone so we spent our childhoods shuttling between their homes and the homes of aunts and uncles and grandparents. Even if someone had put an instrument in my hands, I suspect it would have been for naught. All of the elements that Shinichi Suzuki insisted on were absent: consistency, practice, discipline, support, and environment.

As an adult, I was trying to give my child everything I missed. Perhaps the cello was just a symbol. Was all this healthy? Was I simply displacing my own needs? Was I projecting onto Judah my own unfinished business with my parents? Was I trying to live through my child? Was I trying to make my dreams his dreams? Was I being entirely selfish?

Not entirely, I thought, because there was one other element in play here: guilt. In some ways I had let my older children down by not always being there for them musically. Shira and I made sure they had exposure to music and instruments but I never became their Music Dad.

The reasons for that were understandable. The years when Adam and Emma were six, I was a daily newspaper reporter, a job that often took me away from home and away from the family. At those times I was working at the Times Square newsroom and I worked what I like to call 24/6. (I am a Sabbath observer so I usually managed to take off on the seventh day.) I was building a journalism career, and that meant regularly missing family dinners and, when I was at dinner, taking calls then and at all hours. Taking calls in the 1980s meant something quite different than it does today when cell phones and laptops are ubiquitous.

On a good day in the eighties, I would meet my deadline, leave the office at six, get on a train to our house in suburban New Rochelle, and be home by seven. From six to seven I was what we called "out of pocket," meaning that if my editors had any questions, they couldn't reach me until I walked into the house. Shira's first words when I walked through the door were often "call the office." Sometimes I would manage to begin dinner with the family (who had waited my arrival) and then the phone would ring. And if the editor had a question, he just couldn't shoot over the copy onto my laptop. He'd have to read the changes to me word for word. Meanwhile, I would be signaling to Shira and the kids to go ahead without me.

Still, I loved my work. I almost never turned down an assignment. I wrote about murders and robberies and train crashes and other catastrophes. I covered politicians and celebrities and wrote obituaries and book reviews. And I traveled around the country and around the world, including a monthlong stint in southern Africa. And I started my first book during a two-week vacation (during which Shira took the kids to Boston) and finished it on a series of Sundays (when, again, Shira was with the kids). During those years I left the bulk of parenting to Shira. She threw herself into the task with passion, creativity, and joy. Although we lived in the suburbs, Shira did a whole lot more than open the back door and tell the kids to play in the yard. She took them to the storytelling hour at the local public library and then led them through the stacks to pick out books for reading at home. She took them to state parks and fine art museums and gave them each a sketch pad to draw what they saw. She entered contests on radio stations and won free tickets to amusement parks and the circus. And Shira was the Music Mom during those years, taking Adam and Emma for lessons with a wonderful woman named Rosalyn Tobey, who gave them piano lessons in her home studio surrounded by the paintings of her husband, the muralist and painter Alton Tobey.

I was not part of these adventures and often felt left out. I couldn't wait to get back at night to hear about them. I remember coming home to find Shira reading *The Velveteen Rabbit* or *Charlotte's Web* or *Where the Wild Things Are* to Adam and Emma. All three were curled up on the couch, the kids in footsie pajamas, their hair still wet from the bath. They'd look up at me as if to say, "Who's that? Why's he breaking the magic spell?"

By the time Judah was born in 1995, however, my life had changed radically. We had given up our suburban home and moved to Manhattan. Instead of a life of parenting and freelance writing, Shira took a full-time job, first as a publicist and writer, and then as the head of her own public relations and marketing firm. As her professional life became busier and more demanding, mine became more manageable. I quit the newspaper business and, by the time Judah was turning six, I was a tenured professor at Columbia. I had responsibilities, of course: classes to teach, papers to evaluate, faculty meetings to attend, and my own research pursuits. But as a professor I also had summers off. And long holiday weekends. And five weeks

off between the fall and spring semester. I had what inspirational speakers might call "the gift of time." I decided to
make Judah's music education my project.

I HAD BIG DREAMS for Judah. After his lessons
with Laura, I would walk her to the front door of our
apartment, hand her a check, and set a time for the next
lesson. I was so thrilled with the progress she was making
with Judah that I was giving her spontaneous raises. She
started at sixty dollars an hour, but after a few months I
told her she was underselling herself and I gave her seventy. Then I started giving her eighty.

One day, while seeing her out, I had to ask. "So Laura,
how good is Judah?"

"He's good. He's real good," she told me. "And he loves
it so."

"I marvel at the way you encourage him. The support.
The cheers. The standing ovations."

"That's all part of my method," she said with a smile.

"Of course, but, Laura, do you think Judah could be a
professional cellist? I mean, do you think he could get into
a conservatory? Maybe make a career out of this?"

Laura looked at me oddly. She was kind of sizing me up
like she did the first time we met on Broadway. "Ari," she

said patiently and kindly as if she had had this conversation with eager Music Dads before, "he's a boy; a talented boy, but still a boy. Give it time. Now, make sure he practices tonight."

THE INTERSCHOOL ORCHESTRAS
OF NEW YORK

Judah's musical life was divided between the school year, when he took lessons with Laura, and the summer, when he'd go to music camp. He attended a Jewish primary school in the Riverdale section of the Bronx, where his day was already chock-full of subjects. He took all of his regular classes—math, science, social studies, English, gym, and art—plus a heavy complement of religious studies, including Bible, Talmud, and Hebrew. Jewish Day Schools do a lot of things well, but music isn't one of them. While there was some music instruction and a lot of singing, the school did not offer orchestra opportunities like many public and private schools. There was no room full of instruments that kids could try out. The few kids who had serious music instruction were learning with private teachers.

This made Judah and his cello rather exotic in the

school. Even in third and fourth grades, Judah was known in school as "the cellist." And, frankly, he loved to flaunt it. He'd carry it to school assemblies with pride.

Still, being the only cellist at his school wasn't ideal for Judah's musical education. He needed to play with others. When he was in sixth grade, the mother of a young violinist in his school told us about an organization called the InterSchool Orchestras, which ran seven performing musical groups in New York City. Judah auditioned for ISO's youngest group, known as the Morningside Orchestra, and was given a seat in the cello section. Unlike me, auditions, rehearsals, or playing in public did not faze him. He was a natural.

Rehearsals for the Morningside Orchestra were held every Tuesday at four o'clock, which made sense for children in public and private schools, but not for Judah, whose school day ended at a quarter past four. After pleading for some early release time, I got Judah excused from his last period at school and took it upon myself to pick him up each Tuesday at three thirty.

I had my routine. On Tuesday mornings I'd bring Judah's cello to work with me and, at the end of the day, drive with it to pick him up at his school. His eyes would light up when I arrived to get him, although I couldn't be sure if he was excited about playing in the Morning-side Orchestra or getting out of school early. Then we'd race downtown in time for him to unpack his cello and be ready for rehearsal.

The Morningside Orchestra was a wonder to behold. Little kids—ranging from seven to thirteen—were ar-ranged in a semicircle facing their conductor, a cheerful, pudgy, and often ebullient man named Robert Johnston. This group of children had all the hallmarks of Upper West Side of Manhattan privilege: braces, pigtails, de-signer knapsacks, cell phones, school uniforms, and a gaggle of nannies and parents who waited patiently dur-ing the rehearsals. Each child held an instrument, often in the half or three-quarter size. There were violins, cellos, flutes, clarinets, and one oboe. The conductor kept them engaged and amused with corny and self-deprecating humor.

"Measure seventy-one," he'd call out, signaling the point in the score where he wanted the orchestra to begin. "Measure seventy-one! My age!" In fact, Robert was barely forty, but the line always got a laugh.

"You're sounding lethargic," he said one night, and then went about defining the word by sticking out his stomach and lolling around the front of the room like a stuffed monster who, he explained, just ate a huge Thanksgiving meal. "Okay," he'd say when the laughter died down. "Measure 161. I said Measure 161! My IQ."

One day Robert handed out the score for a new piece of music, a lyrical composition by Carl Strommen called "Irish Song," and asked the group to sight-read the music as he conducted. The piece was beyond their abilities and the young musicians quickly got lost. Robert stopped. "What's the most important thing about sight-reading?" he asked, hands on his hips.

The youthful orchestra members called out answers.

"Rhythm?" one little girl asked tentatively.

"No!" he shouted.

"Sound?" another ventured.

"No!"

"Intonation?"

"No!"

"Melody?"

"No! No! No!" he said, pounding his music stand. "The most important thing about sight reading is *courage*. You have to have courage!

"Now let's try it again—and this time with *courage*. Ready? Measure sixteen . . . my shoe size."

The rehearsal hour flew by. And every week, the kids got better and better.

AVERY FISHER HALL

Judah's first year with the Morningside Orchestra was the thirty-fifth year since the umbrella organization, the Inter-School Orchestras, was founded. Over the years, many of the young musicians who started with ISO went on to distinguished careers in music, among them the trumpeter with the Canadian Brass, the associate principal cellist at the St. Louis Symphony, the conductor of the Lucerne Symphony Orchestra, the principal bassoonist at the Philadelphia Orchestra, and a timpani player at the Chicago Symphony Orchestra.

ISO was celebrating the anniversary by holding a gala benefit concert at Avery Fisher Hall at Lincoln Center. While ISO parents like me were dazzled that our children were going to have such an opportunity, the significance of playing on the great stage at Avery Fisher, home to the New York Philharmonic, was lost on most of the children. The New York Philharmonic is the orchestra of Leonard Bernstein, Gustav Mahler, Leopold Stokowski, Arturo Toscanini, and Zubin Mehta. All the great cellists I revered played on this stage, including Casals, du Pré, Rostropovich, and, most of all, Mr. J.

I was blown away by the thought of the impending concert.

Like the old joke about Carnegie Hall, there is only one way to get to Avery Fisher and, that is, "practice, practice, practice." Robert put the children through their musical paces again and again and again. They rehearsed "Overture for Orchestra" by the twentieth-century Czech-American composer Vaclav Nelhybel, a piece called "Engines of Resistance" by the contemporary American composer Larry Clark, and the Finale from Beethoven's Fifth Symphony. The children played the music to death. Stopped. Started. Got lost. Got found. Laughed. Joked. And played it again.

More than thirty hours of orchestra practice for what amounted to barely fifteen minutes on the Avery Fisher stage. And that, of course, does not include all the hours and hours of practice that each child prepared on his or her own.

The night of the concert was a triumph. Judah's orchestra began with its three musical offerings, and then the more advanced musical groups in the InterSchool Orchestras took over, playing increasingly sophisticated works with greater confidence and musicianship. It was an evening of Stravinsky, Beethoven, Wagner, and Verdi, all played by the young musicians of the InterSchool Orchestras. But for me nothing equaled the moment in which the smallest players, Judah among them, came out onto the Avery Fisher stage at the end of the evening to join all the musicians in a chorus of "America the Beautiful."

As I watched my son on stage, I thought of another evening almost forty years ago in this same hall. It was 1970 and it wasn't called Avery Fisher yet—that happened in 1973 after Fisher, an amateur violinist who made his fortune inventing and marketing stereo equipment, donated $10.5 million to refurbish what was then simply called Philharmonic Hall. I was twenty and was seated between my mother and a man she was dating, at a performance of Beethoven's famous mass called the *Missa Solemnis*.

Jack knew a great deal about classical music and during one of our first meetings, he grilled me on my tastes. I told him that I liked "light" classical, such as Mozart, Handel, and Tchaikovsky. I didn't really know what I was talking about since my exposure to Mozart was *Eine kleine Nachtmusik,* Handel meant *Messiah,* and Tchaikovsky meant the *1812 Overture*.

Then I dug myself even deeper by adding, "Tell you the truth, I can't stand the heavy stuff like Beethoven, Bach, and Brahms."

Jack furrowed his brow and announced, "That's because you don't know them."

"Judy," he called to my mom, "I've got to educate this boy."

The night of the *Missa Solemnis* concert, Jack bought three tickets. My mother and I went to the Philharmonic together, took our seats, and, as the lights were dimming, Jack slid into the seat next to me.

The music was indeed "heavy." Beethoven began this solemn mass—one of several he wrote—in 1819 to honor of one of his patrons, the Archduke Rudolf who was being installed as a cardinal of the Roman Catholic Church. The story goes that Beethoven was so obsessed with this symphony that he missed the deadline to perform the work at the installation. Instead, the *Missa Solemnis* was first performed in 1824 in St. Petersburg. It is a grand and ambitious work that makes great demands on its soloists, chorus, orchestra—and audience. This is about as heavy as it gets, and, yet, I felt myself drawn into its spectacle and majesty. My eyes scanned the stage and I took in the violinists, the flutists, the French horn players, and the percussionists with their cymbals, timpani, and drums. But I kept coming back to the cellists and their beautiful instruments. I could isolate the sound—the deep, dark, and rich timbres of the cello—and thought it the most wondrous on the stage. If any instrument spoke to me, this was it.

But even more powerful that night was the drama unfolding around me. I had not met many of my mother's suitors in the years since her divorce and this night's circumstance was most unusual. After the concert, Jack took my mother's hand and said, "A pleasure to meet you, Miss Goldman." He then turned and was off. My mother and I went home alone.

A short time later, Jack married my mother. They were married for twenty-five years until my mother's death from cancer in 1995. Over the years, Jack, a physicist and successful corporate executive, was very good to me. He supported me financially (through grad school and until I landed my first job) and he encouraged me in my career as a reporter. He would sometimes proudly show to his friends an article I wrote and call me not his "stepson" but his "son." And, as he had done with "heavy" classical music, Jack enriched my intellectual and social skills in ways that helped me in my personal and professional lives.

As I watched Judah on the stage in 2007, I wished my mother could have seen this: her grandson playing cello at Avery Fisher Hall. For now, I focused on the music. As I had done so long ago in this hall, I took in all the wonders of the orchestra—the violins, the woodwinds, the percussion section—until I came again to the cellos. And there, among the players, was Judah, playing the music that spoke to me on this night in a whole new way.

THE OLDEST KID IN THE ORCHESTRA

After his Avery Fisher debut, Judah signed up with the youth orchestra for another season and then I hatched a plot. Simply put, I was jealous. I, too, wanted to play in an orchestra. I had had a few experiences with amateur orchestras in my twenties but I found that the conductors had little patience with rookies. To make matters worse, I had hardly touched a cello in years, unless you count a few failed efforts to jump-start my cello playing. Most of my contact with the cello was carrying and unpacking Judah's instrument. I went to our storage closet, fished out my old cello, and gave it the once over. It was Bill, the beat-up student cello that Mr. J sold to me for five hundred dollars in 1976. Now, with the passage of time, it looked even worse. It suffered from the years of neglect and the vagaries of New York apartment living where heat seemed to be coming out of the old radiators in all four seasons. The cello's bridge, the fine wood structure that held up the strings, had collapsed. There were hairline cracks in the wood and some of the joints—the places where two pieces of wood came together—had separated. Like many aging beauties, my cello was in need of reconstructive surgery. Mr J used to talk about his cello repairman as his "luthier," from the French word *luth* or lute. A luthier makes and repairs string instruments like violins, cellos, and guitars. This was certainly a job for a luthier, and I sought out my very own at a violin repair shop near Lincoln Center. The proprietor took one look at my ailing instrument and dismissed it out of hand.

"It would cost you more to fix that than you paid for it," he told me without even asking me how much I paid for it. And then, turning up his nose, he added: "I don't fix student cellos."

"How much," I asked him, reasoning that even luthiers must have their price. "Fifteen hundred," he told me.

Sparsamkeit erhalt das haus, I heard Mr. J say. *Frugality keeps the house. Move on. You can get a new one for less.*

But it connects me to you, I heard myself responding. *I need to keep trying to get the sound out of it that you did.*

Mr. J did not argue.

"Fifteen hundred it is," I said. The luthier, fearing I would never come back, made me pay up front.

MR. J'S OLD CELLO restored, I needed a teacher.
Judah was doing so well with Laura that I asked her if she
would be willing to spend an extra hour at our apartment
on Sunday mornings teaching me.

"How tough do you want me to be on you?" Laura
asked at our first lesson. Although it was obvious, I told
her that my goals for myself and my goals for Judah were
quite different. "I think he can be great. As for me, I just
want to make music."

I had no illusions about what I could do on the cello. I
remember once joking with Mr. J that I was going to quit
journalism and spend full time on my instrument. Apparently that was not something to joke about. "That's not a
good idea, Ari," he said sternly. "Being a musician is a very
hard life. Besides, you have a profession. Let us just play
for the love of it."

I wanted to be sure that Laura understood that, too. I
knew that she was an exacting teacher. I saw the way she
worked with Judah. I told her that she did not have to cor-
rect my every missed note and wrong bow direction. "Go
easy on me."

Laura and I went over the basics of holding the instrument and doing the C scale. She was pleased I knew as

much as I did. "You had a good teacher," she said admiringly. After some more preliminaries, Laura and I settled on a piece that I could comfortably play, Minuet no. 3 by Bach, the last song in the first Suzuki book.

Judah took my first lesson with Laura as an opportunity to turn the tables on me. I had sat in on his lessons for so long, now he sat in on mine. "I think you should start with 'Twinkle,'" he said, referring to the first song in the first Suzuki book. "No shortcuts!" He was just drawing on his own experience with Laura. She would not let him go on to the next piece in the Suzuki book until he mastered the one he was working on.

I was caught, but came up with something of a rejoinder.

"I'm learning it the Hebrew way," I told him with a weak smile. "We start at the end of the book." Satisfied, Judah lost interest and went off to his room.

Laura and I got off to a good start, but progress was slow. I was trying to get back my game and take it a step further. As I began to play again, I remembered all over again how the art of making music involved so many moving parts: the cello, the bow, the fingers, the hands, the strings, the bridge, the pegs, not to mention the other elements Mr. J emphasized: the body, the voice, and the mind. I found that I could get some of them right, but not all of them right at the same time.

With a few weeks of lessons under my belt, I felt confident enough to approach Judah's conductor, Robert, and asked if I could play with the Morningside Orchestra. Much to my surprise, he was receptive to the idea. "You'll be the oldest kid here," he told me with a smile. All my fears about not being good enough faded away. Here, at last, was a conductor who liked rookies. Best of all, Robert didn't even make me audition. I asked and was instantly admitted.

Even now, all these years later, I marvel at how easy it was. After all, if this had been Little League or the school play or the science fair, I'm sure I would have been shown the door. How absurd for an adult to join any of those activities—and how potentially suspicious. But here I was given complete trust. I was supremely grateful. Robert could have told me to find an adult orchestra, to play with people my own age. But this was even better. What better place to restart my unfulfilled cello ambitions than in a youth orchestra?

And so, in my late fifties, I became the oldest member

of Morningside, the youngest music group of the Inter-School Orchestras. Judah, who was then twelve, was cool with my joining. A year later that might not have been the case, but the sullenness of adolescence had not yet kicked in with my youngest son. I was not (yet) the embarrassment I was destined to become.

What's more, Judah even let me sit next to him in the cello section! Still, while Judah was happy to have me nearby, the conductor did not think that was a good idea. "A large part of being in an orchestra is socialization," Robert explained after I spent a couple of sessions sitting next to Judah. "So we are going to mix things up," he said. However, I suspect there were other factors at play. After all, Robert didn't need a six-foot-tall adult sitting in the front row, blocking out all the little kids. Obediently, I took a seat in the back, sharing a stand with a confident fifth grader named Francesca who, when I got lost in the score, was kind enough to point out the place where I should be.

One of the first lessons about being in an orchestra with children was this: I needed more practice than they did. Orchestral playing came a lot easier to Judah than it did to me. In truth, he never practiced the orchestra music during the week—he was working instead on the solo pieces

that he was learning with Laura—but I desperately needed
to practice. In fact, Laura and I spent most of our lessons
preparing for the Morningside Orchestra rehearsals.

Among the pieces the orchestra was preparing that season were selections from Holst's *The Planets* and Rimsky-
Korsakov's *Snow Maiden*. I was having an especially hard
time with the sixteenth notes in *The Planets*. They were
itty-bitty sounds that suddenly came bursting out of all
the instruments around me. I heard them, I could even
sing them, but my bow and fingers just wouldn't move fast
enough to play them.

Just play the first note of each bar, Mr. J whispered in
my ear. *The important thing is to keep up a steady rhythm.
Stopping is not an option.*

Robert spent a good deal of time on dynamics, especially when it came to the Holst piece. *Dynamics is your
volume control button,* Mr. J reminded me. *You can turn it
up or you can turn it down.* In a piece of music, dynamics
are indicated by markings centered on two terms, piano
and forte, indicated in the music by *p* and *f.* But there are
more subtle variations like mezzopiano (*mp*), which is
moderately soft, and mezzoforte (*mf*), moderately loud.
But why deal in moderation when you can deal in ex-
tremes, like music noted *ppp* (as soft as possible) and *fff*

(as loud as possible). *The Planets* by Holst, asks for even more, ***ffff,*** which I guess means even louder than possible. What a great piece to play with a bunch of kids. We got as noisy as we could without ever losing the music.

Louder! Louder! Mr. J was now shouting in my ear. *To get louder, check your ninety-degree angle. It's not about pressing hard. It's about the ninety degrees. The bow must be at a ninety-degree angle to the string.* He stood in front of me. I saw his familiar face and his strong hands, but his body had become a full-length mirror. *Look in the mirror! Is your bow at a ninety-degree angle to the strings? Looks like fifty to me. Okay. Now, sixty, seventy, eighty. You've got it! Ninety degrees. And your sound! Forte-fortissimo!*

THERE WAS NO BIG Lincoln Center gala planned the year I joined ISO as there had been for the thirty-fifth anniversary. Instead we played at a smaller and funkier venue called Symphony Space, a performing arts center on Manhattan's Upper West Side. To me, though, the venue hardly made a difference. I was about to experience playing cello with an orchestra before an audience in a proper concert hall.

There was great anticipation and excitement on the night of the concert even though we had the most forgiving of audiences: parents, siblings, and friends. Shira was there in her dual roles. While many of the orchestra members had mothers in the crowd, I was the only one with a wife sitting there.

We boys wore black pants, white shirts, and ties and the girls wore knee-length dark skirts and white blouses. Though I did my best to blend in, I felt that I stood out like Mr. Johnson's lethargic Thanksgiving monster. Still, I played, surrounded by beautiful, if not perfectly executed, music. Of course, we made some mistakes but you wouldn't have known it from the audience's reaction. We were praised, cheered, applauded, and lauded. I loved the warm embrace of the crowd, but perhaps the greatest compliment came when Judah and I were packing up our cellos backstage after the concert. "Nice going, Dad. I knew you could do it."

PART FOUR

THE NEW YORK LATE-STARTERS STRING ORCHESTRA

Had I learned to fiddle, I should have done nothing else.
—SAMUEL JOHNSON

A fter my season with the kids at the Morningside Orchestra, I wrote a feature article for my old newspaper about playing music with Judah called BIG CELLO, LITTLE CELLO. Underneath the title ran this momentous line: "For months, he watched his young son play. Then he took a seat beside him." With that, the invitations started to pour in. I heard from numerous orchestras in New York—and around the country—inviting me to join.

This is the moment you've been waiting for, Mr. J exhorted. *Seize it!*

I remembered that after his retreat from the limelight, Mr. J conducted community orchestras, one at the Music Conservatory of Westchester and the other at the Armonk Village School of Music. *The musical world is much bigger than the philharmonics. Seize it!*

Most of the orchestras that got in touch with me after the article appeared seemed out of my reach, some because of geography and others because of the skill level required, but one, the New York Late-Starters String Orchestra, seemed plausible. "I think you'll fit in here," read the note from one of the cofounders, Elena Rahona. I would come to know her as a bright, blue-eyed, bubbly, and athletic AIDS researcher in her early thirties.

Elena is your classic late starter. She was born in Boston, the daughter of a sales and marketing manager for an international hotel chain, and, as she put it, grew up "up and down the East Coast"—from Massachusetts to New York to Florida to Vermont to Washington, D.C.—as her father's work shifted locales. The thread through her childhood was sports, which helped her cope with each move the family made. "I knew that wherever I was, I could join a team. I was good. Someone would have me." Elena played competitive soccer for nearly twenty-five years. "And when I wasn't at practice I would be running or lifting weights or doing drills in my backyard."

It wasn't until after college that she picked up the violin. Elena waxed eloquent when I asked her about her choice. "There was always a part of me that loved the way it sounded, the way it could evoke emotions," she said, adding: "I was curious about what it must be like to be the one creating the happiness . . . or the sorrow or the anger" that the violin expressed.

"I also thought somehow that if I could just make that music, I would never be sad, or rather, I would be, but if I had the power of making the music myself, all I would have to do is pick up my violin and in a few minutes, create joy. Of course I didn't know that it would be years and years of lessons before I would be able to come close to that."

Elena found a teacher, and, after just a couple of years of playing, she was scouring the Internet for a musical community at her level. She came across a summer program run by a British organization called the East London Late Starters Orchestra. She sent them an e-mail. "It was the best 'send' button I ever hit," she told me. The group, known by its letters, ELLSO, was started in the early 1980s by a group of parents who brought their kids to music lessons week after week and realized that the kids were having all the fun. They wanted some of that, too. The parents decided to organize a musical experience for themselves under the ELLSO banner. Almost thirty years later, many of those children no longer play, but ELLSO members still meet with their violins and cellos weekly in

London during the academic year. In the summers, they host a musical retreat program in the north of England. Elena signed up.

"The first time I ever played with anyone it was at ELLSO in 2005," she told me one day when we met at a Starbucks in New York's financial district. "I was so new that I forgot I was supposed to sit down when I played!" She gave an embarrassed laugh. "I always practiced standing up. But then I looked around and everyone was sitting. So I sat, too."

Elena loved the experience in England—"one of the great ways to spend a week," she said—and met many new friends, people she soon came to consider her English family. The intimacy of music making, even without words exchanged, can sometimes do that, especially with your "stand partner," the person who shares a page of music with you. "There is an instant level of trust that stand partners are compelled to establish. The vulnerability felt in the cozy confines of the teacher's studio must all of a sudden be shared with a person you may have met only minutes before. And if this is true for experienced players, how much more for late starters.

"Everyone is very encouraging and forgiving," she said. "Rather than slink down in your chair and make as little noise as possible, the late-starting group provides a safe environment where it is okay to let down your guard and let the music flow."

While most of her new friends were Brits, she also made friends among other international players. She became particularly close to a late starter from Italy and another from Russia. The three of them were the foreigners at ELLSO that summer and, at one point, sat down with Chris Shurety, who was among that initial group of envious parents in the 1980s. One of his children was playing the cello back then, so he decided to try a string instrument as well. He picked up the violin. Now, all these years later, Chris urged the three foreigners to carry the ELLSO gospel to their countries. "We've got to take this international," Chris said.

Elena gave it some thought upon her return to New York but the idea never got off the ground. When she returned to the summer program for a second year, Chris asked: "Any progress? You know you've got to do this." By this time, another American had come to the program, a fellow New Yorker named Andrea Lockett, an editor, writer, and poet who, like Elena, was in her thirties and had discovered the violin after college.

Andrea, petite and intense, grew up in a suburban

New Jersey town and spent a lot of time in the home of
her grandparents. She loved to lose herself in their library, which had six thousand books on a wealth of subjects, and she became a voracious reader. Like Elena, she
played competitive sports in school but, unlike her new
friend, she had considerable exposure to piano and flute
as a youngster. She could read music, but sports won out.
Andrea spent most of her school years fencing and playing lacrosse. "Team sports were a lot more fun than doing
scales and drills," she said.

Andrea went off to the University of Pennsylvania
where she studied English and worked on literary magazines. After college she wrote for medical journals and
pharmaceutical companies. That kind of work "paid the
bills" but her literary side was unfulfilled. She wrote poetry and volunteered at literary journals. She eventually
became an editor of the *New York Quarterly*, which pub-
lishes poetry. Yet, her musical muse was also calling. She
took up guitar at thirty-three and violin at thirty-eight.

Andrea told me about her musical life when we met at
a café in Greenwich Village. She had just dropped off her
young son at a day care program in a nearby church. In a
story that was becoming increasingly familiar as I asked
people about their music teachers, Andrea told me that

she found her violin teacher, a Juilliard student named Alexandra, on Craigslist. After making contact, the two agreed to meet for their first lesson at the practice studios at the prestigious music school.

Andrea remembered approaching the Juilliard building with a sense of awe. She imagined all the great musicians who had walked those halls—and then she saw one of them. Coming out of a classroom as she was passing by was Itzhak Perlman. "Of course Perlman is immediately recognizable, with that wonderful mass of curly hair and broad smile," she recalled. Perlman, a childhood victim of polio, was in a wheelchair and surrounded by students. "It was already exciting to be in the building, but that close encounter with Perlman was both humbling and electrifying. I was still learning how to control my bow and keep my violin from slipping off my shoulder. At the same time, I was casually walking through a space next to one of the most passionate and dedicated violinists of our time, an artist who has made a career of playing a challenging instrument despite his own physical challenges."

Some people might have been daunted by the encounter but Andrea was inspired. She dove into her Suzuki Book 1, a text written for children, with new vigor and commitment. Barely a year into violin lessons, Andrea went to the ELLSO summer program in England, which provided another boost to her playing. ELLSO is largely made up of British retirees. Instantly, she said, she felt like a celebrity. "People were so welcoming," she said. "They were excited to see a young person. They were excited to see an American. They were excited to see a person of color. They'd meet me on the cafeteria line and say, 'Come, sit at our table.'"

At ELLSO, Andrea also bonded with Elena and they resolved, upon returning to New York, to start a New York version of ELLSO, which they dubbed NYLSO: the New York Late-Starters String Orchestra. They had no conductor, no members, and no place to play, but they were convinced that they had a potent idea. Again they turned to Craigslist. Andrea placed an ad: ADULT BEGINNER STRING ORCHESTRA SEEKS TUTOR. They called the job a "tutor" because they didn't quite have the courage to write "conductor." It seemed presumptuous. After all, they didn't yet have an orchestra; how could they advertise for a conductor?

In the ad, under the section about qualifications, they listed "willing to make a weekly commitment" first and "has basic conducting skills" second. Other qualifications were "understands the difference between working with children and working with adults," and has an ability to work with everyone from "rank beginners" to "experienced amateurs." In return they offered a salary that was to be negotiated later.

A few days later they heard from a young Polish émigré and violinist named Magdalena Garbalinska, who was pursuing her masters in music at the Manhattan School of Music. The two organizers met with Magda at a Greenwich Village restaurant and talked about their dream. "We told her what we liked about ELLSO," Andrea said, "and how we wanted to create a group in New York where people of different ages and different skill levels could enjoy music together. That's a hard thing to create, especially in New York, where people expect the best."

One thing was certain: no kids. There are already many music programs for children in New York and once you bring in children you have to deal with supervision issues and discipline and parents. Adults are motivated in a very different way. And besides, Elena said, kids learn so fast and excel in music. "They'll put us to shame."

Elena was right. There are a number of "intergenerational orchestras" in the United States that bring together young and old musicians. I attended a concert of one such group in New Jersey not long ago and actually felt sorry for the old folks. The kids were dazzling. The elderly plodded along. I didn't want to be one of them. (I actually wanted to be one of the kids, but it was too late for that.)

Magda felt very much in sync with the NYLSO organizers. "I thought it went well," Magda told me when I asked her about that initial meeting, "but then I didn't hear from them for weeks and weeks so I thought they found someone else."

There was no one else — Magda was the only applicant they interviewed — but Elena and Andrea were plagued by self-doubt. Neither was making a lot of money and both wondered if this was the best way to spend their energies. Indeed, they asked themselves, "Why are we hiring a conductor when we don't have an orchestra?"

They put a new ad in Craigslist, this one for musicians interested in joining — they decided to limit the group just to string players — and were surprised when over thirty people responded. Reassured, they called Magda and signed her up.

A dozen players of various abilities showed up for the first meeting. "It was a disaster," Magda remembered. There was everything from the conservatory dropout to the cellist who didn't know how to tune his instrument. It was actually worse than that. He didn't even know that the cello had to be tuned. One woman came with a violin but never raised it to her chin. She sat and strummed it like a guitar. Another woman clipped her nails during breaks in the rehearsal and yet another nervously handed out snacks.

The first few meetings were demoralizing, evoking doubt yet again. Players at first came and went, but after a couple of months, a core group began to develop. Then, as they were getting the operation off the ground, Andrea became pregnant. It was left to Elena to work things out with Magda.

Elena and Magda are two very different personality types. Elena is girlish and downright silly at times. When the music goes awry in the orchestra—as it has a tendency to do—Elena is the first to laugh. It starts as a giggle but then morphs to a shoulder-shaking laugh that spreads to her stand partner and soon to the whole violin section. Magda, on the other hand, is strict, serious, and demanding.

"I sometimes feel bad," Elena says. "From Magda's point of view, here we are taking something sacred—music—and desecrating it."

"Okay. What's so funny? I once asked Elena. She suddenly got serious. "It's not that I do not believe that music is sacred. On the contrary, I can rightly say that I am utterly in awe of its powers. I think I laugh because laughter helps remedy what could be a very frustrating experience. Once I realized (basically after my first violin lesson) that I wouldn't suddenly be making happy music—that this was going to be a long, long road of scratches and squeaks—I decided that the only way I would be able to enjoy the learning process was to laugh a little. I've come to relish the flubs and give myself permission to pursue something I have no hope of ever mastering."

Anyway, she thinks laughter is better than being overly self-critical. That, she added, would only lead to becoming bitter and flustered and, worse, giving up.

Unlike Elena and the Late Starters, Magda was classically trained from a very young age. She was born in the western Polish town of Szczecin, near the German border, and began violin at the age of six. "It fit me right away," she said of the instrument. "My mother had this huge dream of becoming a musician but she never got to do it. She pushed me very hard to play and practice."

Szczecin was a great place to practice. Magda grew up in the waning days of Communism and, as she recalled, "There were very few diversions. We had only two TV channels . . . I practiced all the time." Magda excelled at the violin and, while in high school, was sent to Warsaw to further her studies. There, under the guidance of a demanding teacher, she studied Beethoven's violin concerto. But she soon locked horns with her teacher over the proper musical interpretation of the piece. At this time, Poland was opening up politically and friends suggested that she continue her studies in the United States. Magda heard about a Polish violinist who was teaching at the music program at Western Michigan University in Kalamazoo, applied to that program, and was accepted. In Kalamazoo she fell in love and married another musician, an American jazz bassist named PJ.

It was PJ, in fact, who first saw the Craigslist ad for a NYLSO "tutor" soon after the couple moved to New York. Magda was in school, and PJ, a freelance musician, was just beginning to find work. PJ thought this would be a great job for Magda and a good way to supplement the family income. He urged her to apply.

Working with LSO has been part of the continuing process of the Americanization of Magda. "I am just getting used to the idea that it's okay not to be perfect," she said in something of an understatement. The core group that began to develop at LSO were eager, to be sure, but far from polished. What's more, they were old, or at least older than Magda, who was barely thirty. Suddenly, she said, she was in the position of "bossing around people who are my parents' age."

"I come from a cultural setting where if someone is an adult, they are right," she added. "The hard thing for me at LSO is that I'm one of the younger ones. And I'm in charge!"

Early on, the group had its travails. Some Sundays just three or four musicians showed up for a rehearsal. Other Sundays the organizers booked a room only to find that someone else had booked it, too. (Rehearsal instantly cancelled.) But Elena and Andrea and Magda and the New York Late-Starters String Orchestra persevered.

Magda, who is often stiff and unforgiving at LSO rehearsals, seemed happy, relaxed, and at ease when we met to talk in my Columbia office. She's well aware that she comes off as harsh. "It may not always look like it, but I truly enjoy the rehearsals," she told me. Less appealing for her, she said, were the performances that the orchestra puts on several times a year. She prefers to call them "open rehearsals" to which family and friends are welcome. She is not quite convinced that LSO is an orchestra ready for prime time.

Magda told me that she does have one fundamental disagreement with the way that Elena and Andrea run the orchestra. "I do wish there were auditions, not so much for who should be admitted but just so I know where everyone is musically."

"Too intimidating," Elena said when I repeated the suggestion. And then she repeated her LSO mantra: "If you think you can play, you can play."

At times, Elena even goes beyond her mantra. Sometimes she tells people, "Even if you can't play, you can play." On several occasions she has organized what she calls a "Newbie Day," a Sunday afternoon when people come just to explore what it might be like to play an instrument. On those days, "experienced" LSO players (who are already beginners) show visitors how to hold a violin or cello and demonstrate the rudiments of making music. By the end Elena has everyone playing "Twinkle."

In Elena's mind, an instrument is more than a vehicle for making music. It is an agent of transformation. The mere act of taking up an instrument shows people that they can reach beyond their capabilities and even their imaginations. Elena told me about a woman named Sarah, a widow, who hardly went out of her house after her husband died.

A friend dragged her one Sunday afternoon to LSO where she revived an interest in the violin. One day, she agreed to join the group for drinks at Chef Yu. "Last I heard," Elena said, "she had signed up for Match.com."

THE YEAR THAT I joined the orchestra, my sixtieth year, Andrea was still out with her firstborn and Elena took the lead at LSO. This meant everything from choosing the music—finding the score, listening to it on YouTube, and determining if it was something the group could handle—to renting the hall and collecting the fees that players pay. LSO charges eighty dollars for a six-week cycle, although players can also drop in for a single session for eighteen dollars.

Running LSO takes a lot of time and energy but it has its pleasures as well. "Making music does make my work life more bearable," Elena told me. "It's like I have this whole other world that I can retreat to in my head. I love that." Sometimes, she has to bring her violin with her to work in order to make it to lessons or rehearsals on time. "I talk about this a lot with other adult learners, the fact that having an instrument with you automatically makes people assume you are a 'musician,' especially in New York."

And then Elena raised the same question I have been struggling with ever since my first day with LSO: "At what point," she wondered, "do you get to call yourself a 'musician' and not feel like an impostor?"

I know what she means. After one LSO rehearsal, I walked under the marquees of a half dozen Broadway theaters and hopped on the Fiftieth Street crosstown bus. A young woman saw me coming down the aisle with my cello on my back and offered me her seat. I thanked her but explained that it is easier to stand than to take the cello on and off my back in order to sit. "But you must be tired," she insisted. "It's hard playing a matinee. And you have to go back in a few hours to play the evening performance. Right?"

I smiled knowingly and said bravely, "It's okay, I'm used to this."

CONDUCTING

When we meet for rehearsals, Magda has no time for small talk. She spreads her score out on two music stands and keeps her violin on a small table nearby in case she needs to demonstrate something musically. Right after we tune, we play.

Being in tune is essential. An out-of-tune instrument offends the ear, especially a sensitive ear like Magda's. It doesn't take much for a string instrument to slip out of tune (a change in temperature, a bumpy bus ride, a chance encounter in the elevator); that's why musicians are always tuning.

I usually managed to arrive at LSO on time, but one Sunday there was emergency subway track work on the Number 1 train and it took me forever to make it downtown. The orchestra was already playing. I found an empty chair, set up my music stand, took out my cello, and looked over the shoulder of another cellist to see what we were up to. I found the spot in the music and fell in line with the rhythm. At one point, we cellists had to shift to the open C string and that's when I heard it: my C was woefully out of tune. That long commute had apparently taken its toll.

I wanted to sing out, as Mr. J had taught me, but I wondered if I could do it by ear alone, like the pros do. *Get the sound in your head,* Mr. J said. *Sing, but silently this time.* I reached for the fine tuner—that little knob below the bridge—but I realized that we were talking about major surgery here, not fine-tuning. I lifted my right hand to the top of the cello, known as the scroll, and gave one of the pegs a sharp twist as I plucked the string. Bingo! My C was back in tune. I felt like a pro! Beaming, I joined my fellow musicians.

The next piece was by Carl Nielsen, an early twentieth-century composer. We started together, but then Magda singled out the cellists for special attention. "It starts with an E," she said. "I am hearing an A. Who is playing an A?"

My heart sank. I was busted, exposed for being the musical fraud that I was. But just then, a woman in the front of the cello section fessed up. "It was me. I'm sorry, my strings keep slipping. Must be the weather." I breathed a silent sigh of relief. But just to be sure, I double-checked my note and sang along to be sure. It was an E, after all. I had tuned right and stayed in tune.

Magda, of course, worried about notes, but even more than the notes, she cared about rhythms. In one piece by Edvard Grieg we were having a particularly rough time. She told the violins to put down their instruments and clap out the rhythms while the cello section kept playing the base line. "Again," she said. "And again." She had us do this exercise six times. "That's better," she finally acknowledged.

"Always start with the rhythm, even if you get the notes wrong. Skip the notes, if you must, but keep to the beat." Magda constantly emphasized the importance of *listening* as well as *playing*. "Cellos," she said, addressing us, "you have to *listen* to the violins. Otherwise you run off on your own."

Magda is extremely orderly and precise, but sometimes she surprises us. In the middle of one rehearsal—a rehearsal that wasn't going well—she told everyone to stop, put down our instruments, and stand up. "We are going to rearrange the room," she announced. She made me think of a fifth-grade teacher who was fed up with the class's lack of decorum. If things don't work, shuffle the deck.

Instead of facing her, Magda wanted us to face in different directions at sharp angles to one another. "The only requirement is that no one faces me." Chairs and music stands were soon scattered around the room. "Now find a place, sit down, and play." No one could quite figure out what she was up to. All this was so un-Magdalike.

"The goal," she said, "is not to look at me but to *listen* to each other. Now play."

It is tough playing without seeing the conductor, but we did, guided by the music rather than our leader. It was disorienting, but a valuable lesson.

After a few more tries at it this way, she grouped us once again by instruments and we faced her. We tried it again. "We are getting there," Magda said. "Of course you must *watch* me, but most of all you must *listen* to each other."

Before a performance, Magda was especially inspiring. "Be confident," she told us. "You should have no doubts. Believe in yourself."

You rehearsed it and you know it well. Confidence!

Sometimes her words mingled in my mind with those of Mr. J. There were times I couldn't tell them apart.

Do not be timid. Just play. Express yourself. Think about the sound, the music, the colors. Don't worry that you will miss a fingering or a bow direction. If you skip a note, no one will know. It is about the character of the music.

"Be confident. And look confident," Magda said. "Articulate each note. Good actors in the theater don't mumble. They articulate each word. Articulate."

And even if you don't feel confident," she said, "look confident."

If you look frightened, the audience will only feel bad for you, Mr. J agreed.

"Now give them something they will remember," Magda added.

There was one performance where, despite the pep talks, the first violins were not convinced. In the hour before the performance, when we were having our final rehearsal, Magda demonstrated a particularly difficult passage in a Vivaldi piece, the "Spring" movement from *The Four Seasons*. She played it once with the first violins and then with the whole orchestra. "Now, play it yourselves," she instructed. But the first violins went awry.

"I think we need you at the concert," said a violist named Ron.

"People aren't coming to hear me, they're coming to hear you," Magda said. "You are on your own."

But when we got to the Vivaldi at the performance, Magda took pity on us. She pivoted to the side so that she half faced the audience and half faced us and she played the Vivaldi while conducting with her head and eyes. She was magnificent.

And we sounded pretty good, too.

NISHANTI

The LSO members I played with came from all different backgrounds. While Elena was a true late starter, coming to the violin after college, Andrea was a returning late starter, someone who read music and played an instrument as a youngster, gave it up for years, and then came back to it later in life. Perhaps Nishanti, a woman in her thirties, had the most enchanting story.

Nishanti was born in Sri Lanka and moved to the United States when her father, an emergency room physician, found work in rural Pennsylvania. Nishanti took piano lessons as a child and picked up the violin in elementary school and played through high school. But, she told me, she associated the violin "with being a kid" and left it home when she went off to college. Hers was a long route through college with time off to waitress, it seemed, "in every coffee shop in Pittsburgh." She graduated college in her late twenties and made her way to New York, and eventually found work in financial operations on Wall Street, where she developed a specialty in derivatives. When I commented that it must have been exciting work, she said, "I didn't particularly enjoy my job. In fact, I hated it. It got to the point where I was crying at my desk every day."

It was a stable, if unhappy, place to work, but then an opportunity arose. One day she learned that her company, RBS, was moving to Stamford, Connecticut, and she was one of the lucky ones who was promised continued employment and asked to make the move. But there was another good offer on the table: "A really good exit package." She took the latter and never looked back.

"I quit my job and I made this decision that I was only going to do things that I love to do. No more doing things that I hated. Like finance."

And then the uncanny happened. One day Nishanti was waiting at a bus stop in Brooklyn with her gym bag. "I saw this woman across the street with a cello on her back," she reminisced. "The cello! I'd always wanted to play the cello! So I made a deal with myself. If she walks this way I will ask her about her cello. I will ask her to teach me. And then I will dedicate my life to the cello. If, however, she walks in the opposite direction, then it wasn't meant to be."

Nishanti articulated to me her inner monologue. "Wow. She's walking this way. She's really walking this way. This was meant to be!"

"Then I saw my bus coming. I didn't want to miss it. I was going to the gym. So I accosted her. 'Do you just play or do you also give lessons?' I asked her quickly. 'I do both,' she told me. I quickly took her contact info and hopped on the bus.

"That was a Friday. I called her after the gym and said, 'I'm not just some crazy lady on the street. I know how to read music. I used to play violin.' She said: 'That's okay. It happens to me all the time.'" The teacher's name was Melina and she told Nishanti where to rent a cello and what music to buy. By Sunday Nishanti had a cello and on Monday she took her first lesson with Melina.

Nishanti didn't quite dedicate her life to the instrument, but she did find her way to LSO. Eventually she had to go back to work but steered away from Wall Street and found a job in the nonprofit sector. Now she has what she describes as "a more balanced life" of work and music.

DAN

Several members of the orchestra were newly unemployed or underemployed. This was not entirely a surprise since, as I was entering my sixtieth year, the United States was entering its greatest economic downturn since the Great Depression. The economy was reeling and unemployment nationwide rocketed to new heights. The Great Recession was upon us and it hit New York particularly hard. In the next two years New York City's unemployment rate would top 10 percent, even higher than the national average.

A lot of LSO members were hurting. For some, music might seem like a luxury. What they needed was work, not recreation. But music provided a refuge. *Music is the best cure for a souring heart,* Mr. J said. I was not sure what it could do for a souring economy, but it could certainly help some people through hard times.

One LSO violinist, a middle-aged man named Dan, had just been laid off from a New York advertising firm when I joined the orchestra. He was fifty and had been at the firm for twelve years, working mostly in ad placement and customer service. Dan's musical journey went back to violin lessons in his fourth-grade class at Riverdale Country School, an exclusive private school in a tony section of the Bronx. It wasn't exactly love at first note. "Like a lot of the kids I couldn't get much more than a squeak out of it," he said of his first violin. "I continued in fifth grade but then I gave up on it and turned to piano." Piano is a pleasure after the violin. You hit a key and you get a note. No squeaks. Dan stayed with the piano through high school and then went off to college in Colorado where he eventually got a degree in piano pedagogy.

He never did much teaching, however. He took advantage of the economic boom of the 1990s and moved to Manhattan. Dan continued to play piano—he still has a 1946 Steinway baby grand in his New York apartment—but music was on the back burner. Eventually he was drawn back to the violin playing of his youth, in part, curiously, because of the computer revolution.

An early devotee of the social networks of AOL, Dan became one of the hosts of a classical music chat site, where people traded tips on musical news and offerings. In one chat, he told an online acquaintance that he fondly remembered playing violin in grade school. "You should definitely pick it up again," his AOL friend urged. "You can get a violin for next to nothing on eBay." This being the early days of eBay, such deals were possible, and before he knew it, he had a bow from a seller in Mississippi and a violin from another in Los Angeles. The whole purchase came to less than two hundred dollars.

In retelling the story, Dan marveled at how this online buddy, someone who he never met, inspired him in a way that a good friend or relative couldn't. A good friend might have said, "Stop being a dreamer," or, "Come on, you're not a violinist, you're a pianist," or, "Don't try to be a jack of all trades." But a stranger on AOL could encourage him to "go for it."

Why did he want to play the violin? "I was always fascinated by the power the string section has in an orchestra," Dan said. "Also, I wanted to see if I could get more than the squeak out of it that I got in fourth grade."

Dan found a violin teacher through a music school in Greenwich Village, where he lives, and began to take lessons. "She was impressed by my musicianship," Dan recalled. "But she said that I had to stop listening with a 'pianist's ears.'"

Pianist's ears. It was a term I hadn't heard since my lessons with Mr. J. And it wasn't a flattering one. For the string player, the pianist takes the easy way out. *The piano lies! For the pianist, the C sharp and the D flat are the same. You get them by striking the same black key. But they are not the same note. You can hear that on a violin. You can hear that on a cello. But you can't hear that on a piano. The piano lies.*

String instruments like the violin and cello have no keys; they just have the musician's fingers. And fingers can do what piano keys cannot. Fingers can find that half-tone, that microtone—that nuance—that can never be achieved on a piano. On a piano, the note higher than a C and lower than a D are the same, but not on a violin or a cello. But you can hear it only if you listen with a violinist's ears. Dan developed his violinist's ear and soon was able to play in community orchestras like LSO.

Dan is not a calm guy. He fidgets. I found this observing him at the orchestra and when we went out one day for dinner at a deli on the Upper West Side. "I had anxiety as a student," he said. "I was smart. I should have done better in school, but I'd freeze up at examinations." Public performance is a real challenge for Dan but that is also one of the reasons he threw himself into orchestral playing. "I realize the value of sitting under pressure where there is a great reward," he explained. "It has taken me some time to get this into my head. Getting on stage is a different ball game. No matter how well it goes in the practice room, this is where the real test is."

Orchestral playing has improved his game. It's a mountain for him to climb but it is worth the ascent. He revels in compliments, like the nod from Magda after playing a Bach fugue. "Exemplary," she said. Dan's elderly parents and his siblings have also come to appreciate his playing and have attended the LSO "open rehearsals." His parents' first reaction was, "What about the piano?" but they've come to appreciate the violin in their son's life.

"The praise I get from all different levels of people has helped me realize that I am definitely an above-average player," Dan said. At this stage in life, he is not after greatness; just above-averageness.

I asked Dan how he could sustain his musical interests in the face of losing his job. Unemployment is not a permanent state for him, he assured me. He's found part-time work as a bartender and is planning to take the actuarial qualifying exam. In the meantime, he's done some downsizing. Rather than violin lessons at the music school, he is taking them at his teacher's apartment, where the fees are slightly lower. Two of the community orchestras he plays with have agreed to waive the weekly charges while he is out of work. He told me that it gladdened his heart to find that "the musical organizations I've been in don't act like the phone company, demanding payment or threatening to cut off service."

"What if things turn worse for you financially," I asked. "Would you sell your baby grand piano? Your violin and bow? What if you had to move to a city that didn't have all the musical enrichment that New York City offers?" As soon as the questions came out of my mouth, I regretted asking them. Sometimes the journalist in me takes over. What passes for a question in an interview is not always polite dinner conversation. But Dan did not seem put off.

"I'd never sell any of my musical possessions," he said emphatically. "My music is my life and I would only sell my instruments to upgrade them, for new instruments. Some things just have to remain in that they're part of one's essence. That's certainly how I've experienced music in my life."

JOE

Another LSO member who'd fallen on hard times was Joe. If Dan was slight and fidgety, Joe was centered, calm, and solid. He was the unofficial leader of the cello section; perhaps not the best player, but certainly the most confident. He was also one of the more striking-looking members. Balding on top, he had straight white hair falling to his shoulders and a neatly trimmed white beard. With a cello in his arms he seemed invincible.

Like Dan, Joe was given the opportunity in grade school to play a string instrument. He chose the cello but when it came time to get his instrument, they were out of cellos and the teacher handed him a violin. "A few years ago when I turned fifty-one, I said, 'I'm probably going to die soon'—anything can happen to us at this age—I must get that cello she never gave me."

Joe turned to eBay and bought what he called "a cheapo cello" which was a big mistake. "It was more of a wooden object in a cello shape." He couldn't afford lessons, so he taught himself. "In some ways, I relied on my old violin lessons. In theory, I thought the transition would be easy. You just take the violin from under the chin and turn it upright."

Joe's big leap in his cello playing came when he was laid off from the design firm where he was working. "I practice every day without fail, between four hours and one and a half hours. I cannot go for a day without practicing."

When I came to know him, Joe was living on Long Island but he was frequently in Manhattan, sometimes to play with LSO and sometimes just to practice in Central Park. He took the train into the city and carried with him his cello, his music, his music stand, and a small wooden stool. He explained that since LSO was soon going to be playing as part of an early summer program called Make Music New York, he thought it would be a good idea to practice in Central Park. Joe would set himself up in one of the park's many arched tunnels under a roadway or footbridge and play. "The sound is incredible" in the tunnels, he said. "I sound like a genius.

"And I get a lot of foot traffic, but since there is no place to sit, nobody stays too long, which is a good thing since my repertoire is not very extensive. I play the same things over and over again."

It soon became clear to me that this was also a chance

for Joe to make some extra money. He puts out a canvas bag for change. How much does he make? "It depends on three things: weather, traffic, and mood."

"Wait," I said. "It doesn't depend on how well you are playing?"

"Not at all. What is important is to make good eye contact, especially with children. Smile at a child and the father will give you a buck. Maintain eye contact with a single woman and she'll put money in the bag." He described one woman who fumbled for her change purse as he played. She got so flustered that when she found it, she simply dumped the contents into Joe's kitty. That was probably his best day in the park. He earned eighteen dollars in two hours.

Playing alfresco is no way to make money. Joe would have made more per hour working at the Gap. Somehow people expect music to be free. On a sunny summer day, passersby will pay for a hot dog or for a balloon for their child but will walk right by the street musician without feeling any obligation.

There's a German expression that Mr. J taught me that exhorts people not to take music for granted: *If you enjoyed the dance, pay the musicians.*

WHEN JUDAH WAS SMALL, we had a succession of live-in nannies from a Christian community called the Bruderhof. Founded in 1920 in Germany, the Bruderhof was a socialist community modeled on the principles of the early followers of Jesus who proclaimed themselves of "one heart and mind, and shared all things in common." Most of all they embraced the teachings concerning nonviolence (they were strict pacifists), faithfulness in marriage (no divorce allowed), and compassion for the poor.

Young women from the Bruderhof normally do not go out in the world to be nannies, but I had developed a special relationship with the community when I was a reporter. I had written several articles about their efforts to open the community to the larger world and, at one point, asked if one of the single women would help us out at home. (By that time, I had left the *Times* and felt there was no conflict in employing someone I had written about.) Eager to give their young people an experience with a Jewish family, the Bruderhof elders sent us one woman after another for five years. While they largely acted as nannies, helping us with the children and household tasks, they were really members of our family.

The Bruderhof way of life shares a lot with the Amish community. When I first met them, the men wore beards and suspenders and the women all covered their hair with print kerchiefs. They did not shun technology the way that the Amish do, but they were wary of it.

In this community, playing an instrument was a great virtue. Communal meals and church meetings always included singing along with the band. Our first nanny, Rebecca, played the auto harp and sang. Another, Susan, played the cello. A third, named Noni, wasn't particularly musical, but she took it on herself to nurture Judah's cello playing. When Judah was in elementary school, he claimed to have stage fright and routinely refused to sing in public or even participate in group performances. But he shed his shyness when he played the cello. Behind his instrument, he was confident, even masterful. There and only there, he loved an audience.

Noni had an idea. One afternoon she and Judah baked a batch of chocolate chip cookies and put them in a tin. Then they grabbed Judah's cello and bow and the two of them went to the Columbia campus and set up a sign that said, "CELLO AND COOKIES: 50¢." Judah played while Noni sold cookies. We were never sure what the main draw was, the cookies or the cello, but they had a successful little business venture going. Judah got more and more comfortable with being the center of attention. And the crowd loved it. It was something of a variation on that German proverb. Perhaps: "If you enjoyed the cookies, pay the musician."

AT ONE POINT, JOE the cellist stopped coming to LSO rehearsals. After a few months, he returned and I asked him what had happened. "My financial situation fell apart," he explained. "I was simply overwhelmed." And there was another reason, he said reluctantly. "I felt that the other cellists were relying on me too much."

There was definite truth to that. When I play with the orchestra, I play the parts I know and skip the parts I don't. Sometimes that means an entire piece. I just sit it out. The better players, like Joe, play every note.

"A lot of people," he said, "were playing 'air cello,' moving the bow back and forth but never engaging the string. It looks like you are playing the cello but you're not. I am!"

Joe wasn't exactly angry. He just thought it wasn't fair. After all, he practiced and practiced. He spoke about going over one passage eight thousand times—and I don't think he was exaggerating. I have to admit that sometimes I would show up for rehearsal (after escaping my job, my students, my family, and my editor) and sight-read my way through. I was part of Joe's problem.

But now Joe was back. His financial situation had improved and he needed the orchestra. "You have to play with others and you have to play for people," he said.

I told Joe that I was glad to see him again but wondered why he chose LSO when there were many other community orchestras he could join. He admitted to liking something about the spirit of LSO. He enjoyed the repertoire, which included a lot of chamber music and string quartets scored for an orchestra, and he appreciated the democratic and open nature of LSO.

"You don't have to audition and you don't have to practice," he said, echoing Elena's guidelines. "That's what makes it so great. And that's also what makes it so terrible."

LSO AND SUZUKI

The Late Starters Orchestra approach that I had signed up for was not all that different from the Suzuki method that had worked so brilliantly for Judah. While Suzuki asserts that every child can learn an instrument, the LSO philosophy is that adults can, too, even into middle and old age. Both programs are essentially anti-elitist: good music is not just for the wealthy or the supertalented; it is within everyone's reach. And many of the same behavioral initiations are there: immerse yourself in the music, learn music as you would a language, surround yourself with it and hang out with others who are learning. A chief difference between the two systems is that we late starters do not have parents who take us to lessons, pay for them, remind us to practice, and cheer us on.

In Suzuki, children are praised at every step—and rightly so. A child's slow, steady mastery of his or her instrument is nothing short of remarkable. When Judah was little—and here I mean six, seven, and eight—we pulled out the cello nearly every time a guest came over. He'd play "Twinkle, Twinkle" and later a straightforward Bach minuet, and the crowd would go crazy. Family and friends seemed to loved it, and whether sincere or not, their applause gave Judah a sense of accomplishment and confidence. One of the first lessons that children learn in Suzuki is how to take a graceful bow and Judah used his often.

But no one is going to rise to their feet after hearing an adult play "Twinkle" or a familiar minuet. More often their reaction is: "That's it? That's what you are spending your time doing? That's what you learned in six months?" But "Twinkle" we must. At any age, music is learned in minute, deliberate steps. And, while we late starters bring a lot to the table in terms of life experience, intelligence, and motivation, we recognize that we can never recapture the plasticity of mind and the luxury of time that comes only in youth. Youth can achieve mastery; the most we can hope for is competence. In his best-selling book *Outliers* Malcolm Gladwell writes that there is no secret to greatness: in a word, it comes from repetition. "Ten thousand hours" is his mantra.

Gladwell argues that everyone—from top hockey players to Olympic ice skaters to world-class chess players to master safe crackers to successful computer geeks to prima ballerinas—put in their ten thousand. Gladwell was criticized for being simplistic on this score when his book came out in 2008. There are, his detractors argue, certainly such factors as talent, health, genetics, environment, economics, parents, and teachers. All of these contribute to greatness, not just slavish practice.

But practice has its virtues. The ten-thousand-hour theory was first advanced by the cognitive psychologist K. Anders Ericsson of Florida State University, who initially studied just what it is that makes a great musician. Ericsson and two colleagues followed violin students at Berlin's Academy of Music. The violinists were grouped into three categories: those who were merely "good," those who were likely to play in professional orchestras, and those who had the potential to become world-class soloists. All of them, the researchers found, started playing at around the age of five. "In those first few years," Gladwell writes of Ericsson's study, "everyone practiced roughly the same amount, about two or three hours a week. But when the students were around the age of eight, real differences started to emerge."

Some maintained their steady two or three hours, but others ratcheted it up year by year until they were practicing more than thirty hours a week by the time they were in their early twenties. The study of these three groups found that the more a student practiced, the greater their chance of being a world-class musician.

"Elite performance," Anders and his colleagues wrote in 1993 in the *Psychological Review,* the journal of the American Psychological Association, is "the product of a decade or more of maximal efforts to improve performance in a domain through an optimal distribution of deliberate practice."

In *Outliers,* Gladwell popularizes this as: "Ten thousand hours is the magic number of greatness." Without it, he says, there is none.

I read this and shudder. I ask: Who at my age has ten thousand hours?

The answer, of course, is no one. But then the goal of the late starter is not to be a virtuoso or prodigy (too late for that), but to be competent. And recent advances in brain science put competence clearly within reach of late starters. As Dr. Doidge explains in *The Brain That Changes Itself*, the science of neuroplasticity is overturning the notion that the human brain, developed in childhood, is fixed for life. Doidge documents the work of a group of physicians and researchers he calls the "neuroplasticians," who "rewire" the brain through behavioral changes and without surgery. He tells of people who are able to move paralyzed limbs or restore vision to blinded eyes because of neuroplasticity. "I met people whose learning disorders were cured and whose IQs were raised," he writes. "I saw people rewire their brains with their thoughts, to cure previously incurable obsessions and traumas."

Examples abound of people late in life not only recovering from handicaps but achieving great things. Golda Meir did not become prime minister of Israel until she was seventy. Noah Webster was sixty-nine when he first published his famous dictionary, and Peter Mark Roget was seventy-three when he published the first edition of his famous thesaurus. Benjamin Franklin was seventy-eight when he invented bifocals, and Frank Lloyd Wright was ninety when he designed the Guggenheim Museum.

It may be too late for late starters to develop the neurons that form extra brain mass in the brains of young musicians, but certainly new pathways into the brain can be created. New skills can be learned. And new instruments played competently if not with mastery, opening up whole new vistas of achievement and enjoyment. And that is what keeps me going.

THE EAST LONDON
LATE STARTERS ORCHESTRA

The group of parents who started ELLSO in 1982 was led by a civil engineer with no musical background named Chris Shurety.

"I will never forget the day my daughter Kate came home with a cello," Chris told me when we met in England. "She was seven years old, she was so pleased. What was wonderful was that she hadn't been singled out; the whole class had been given the chance to take home either a violin or a cello. They'd had a couple of musicians come in and play these instruments, then they said, 'Who wants one?' Everyone put up their hands, and they were each given one to take home."

It was all part of an experimental musical enrichment program in the East London public schools. Soon Chris and other parents were spending their Saturday mornings watching their children make music. "Three or four of us looked at each other and said, 'We could do this!'" On behalf of the group, Chris, who was then working for the City of London, approached the school and asked if there were any instruments left over. The school not only gave the parents instruments but arranged for lessons. The classes, however, were offered on a weekday afternoon, and Chris, being a city employee with a flexible job, was the only one able to attend.

"I went and then taught what I learned to the others," he said. He held his sessions on Saturday mornings while the children played nearby. But ELLSO, as the group came to be known, grew in unexpected ways. A turning point came in 1998 when the Sunday magazine of the *Times* of London published an article. It was written by Rose Shepherd, who chanced upon an ELLSO concert at "Hawksmoor Church off the Highway at Wapping, East London," and declared that "it wasn't half bad." But what happened to her next, Shepherd wrote, was nothing short of remarkable. "After the proper concert anyone from the audience could choose an instrument—violin, viola, cello—and have a bash. Then the whole ensemble launched into the waltz, and the new recruits were free to string along." Shepherd was swept up in the moment. "I plied the bow, I sawed about on open strings . . . and heard something almost tuneful in my left ear. I was reluctant, at first, to get involved. I'm cloth-eared, if not actually tone-deaf (a far more rare condition I am assured, than most of us imagine), and was appalled by the idea of making a public spectacle of myself. But the people were so per-suasive, so supportive, and it had been so long since any-one proposed making beautiful music: in the end, I just couldn't say no."

Shepherd was hooked. "I hadn't 'played' an instrument since, at age five, I banged out 'Oranges and Lemons' on the triangle with my school percussion band, on stage at the Civic Hall, Croydon. To have the chance, even to hold a violin was . . . well what everybody says: a revelation."

She ended her article this way: "You know, you really ought to try it."

They did. "At the first meeting of ELLSO after the ar-ticle appeared, there was a line of people around the block carrying instruments and waiting to get in," said Carol Godsmark, who remembers the scene vividly because she was one of those people. She is now the executive director of the East London group. But back then she was just another aspiring late starter who brought her violin, which she hadn't played since she was a youngster in Czechoslovakia. "Some of those people got up at five in the morning and drove 150 miles to get to London on time."

Today, some two hundred people participate in the East London group on a weekly basis. "There's a very strong amateur tradition in this country," Chris explained. "It grows out of the role of music in the nineteenth century workers' movement. There were certain composers associated with it. These composers wrote music not for the rich but for the working folk." Add to that a mandatory retirement age in England of sixty-five and you've got a lot of people with a lot of time on their hands who want to turn their attention to music. Many, of course, find more solitary pursuits, such as gardening, painting, quilting, and even playing the piano, but England is a nation of joiners.

America, on the other hand, is a nation of rugged individualists. In most American professions, there is no official retirement age and, in this economy, even those who can retire often postpone it. And all of this accounts for big differences between amateur music in the United States and England. If, for example, you Google "Making

Music U.K.," you will learn that there are 2,850 voluntary and amateur music groups throughout the British Isles, including choirs, orchestras, samba bands, jazz groups, festivals, handbell ringers, barbershop choruses, brass bands, folk groups, and many others. Making Music is a nonprofit organization that represents and supports these groups.

Then try Googling "Making Music U.S." and you'll find a for-profit organization that books professional musicians for "anything and everything," from a soprano or harpist for "your wedding ceremony" to a brass quintet for a corporate event.

Of course there are many amateur orchestras in the United States. But my point is that the first thing that the music seeker finds in the United States is professional musicians; in the United Kingdom, you find the amateur musicians themselves. It's the difference between doing it yourself and ordering in. When it comes to music at least, we Americans are better at ordering in than playing ourselves.

THE REALLY TERRIBLE ORCHESTRA

Before I wax too poetic about community orchestras, I should point out that there is a downside to them, a caution best expressed by the Irish playwright George Bernard

Shaw, who said, "Hell is full of musical amateurs: music is the brandy of the damned." Shaw was probably referring to the bad fiddlers and fife players of his day who subjected everyone at the pub to their latest jig and reel. But there's a lot of bad amateur music today, too, as one can see in everything from auditions for *American Idol* to the incessant postings of Beatles and Simon & Garfunkel covers on YouTube.

Some amateur groups simply give music a bad name; in fact, one even has it in its name. It is the RTO, the Really Terrible Orchestra. The RTO, based in Edinburgh, Scotland, and made up of middle-aged musicians and late starters, is actually proud of its terribleness. It grew out of the same soil as the East London Late Starters but took a wrong turn somewhere along the way.

One of the RTO's founders and champions is Alexander McCall Smith, the author of the immensely popular No. 1 Ladies' Detective Agency series. As McCall Smith, a rookie bassoonist, tells it, he was among a group of adult players who were "unable to infiltrate" amateur orchestras in Edinburgh. "We shall start our own orchestra!" McCall Smith declared. "It won't be a very good orchestra, in fact it will be a really terrible one."

And so the name was born. The RTO began with ten

players and has grown to sixty-five. Like with the LSO, the RTO has no audition requirement. But unlike the LSO, the RTO takes pride in its limitations. After all, we may call ourselves late, but they call themselves terrible.

The RTO found not only players but an audience. It stages an annual concert in Edinburgh, although these are usually associated with that city's experimental theater event known as the Fringe Festival. After several successful years there, the RTO began a "world tour," which meant a one-night stand on April Fools' Day in New York's Town Hall.

At one LSO rehearsal, Elena, our cofounder and unofficial social director, suggested a group outing to the concert. It sounded kind of campy so I picked up tickets for Shira and Judah. I thought Shira would enjoy meeting some of the LSO members that I had been telling her about. As for Judah, I thought it would show him a lighter, looser, and fun side of classical music that Suzuki didn't often showcase.

About a dozen LSO players came to the RTO concert. I was looking forward to showing off my family and introducing them to Elena and Andrea, who are both in their thirties, to Dan and Joe, both in their fifties, and to my older friends Eve and Mary and Adriana. But I didn't see any of the older folks that night at Town Hall, just some of the younger LSO players.

As the house lights dimmed, the members of the Really Terrible Orchestra began to take their places on stage. They were a bedraggled group that looked like they came directly from the airport. Many orchestras perform in formal wear; this group came out in sweat pants, jeans, and traveling clothes. The only ones dressed for the occasion were McCall Smith, his hair wild but his bow tie in place, and the conductor, Richard Neville-Towle.

After an inordinate amount of time tuning, Neville-Towle raised his baton and the orchestra began playing the final movement of Tchaikovsky's "1812 Overture." It seemed like the time tuning was for naught. There was a familiar melody somewhere in there but it was hard to spot. The audience laughed and applauded, but Judah just slumped in his seat. "They're awful!" he groaned.

"You mean *terrible*," I said. "C'mon, Judah, they're funny." But Judah just sank even lower in his chair and pulled his sweatshirt hood tight around his face.

"Leave him alone," Shira instructed gently. "He's fourteen. He's in the pre-ironic age."

It wasn't just that he was pre-ironic, he was like the little boy in *The Emperor's New Clothes*. The RTO was pretty lame. The orchestra made a stab at one more piece and then the silliness began. Musical selections from *The Sound of Music* were next and the audience was encouraged to clap and sing along. Then it was time for Gilbert and Sullivan, with a Scotsman dressed in a kilt doing a rendition of "I Am the Very Model of a Modern Major-General."

Judah took advantage of the intermission by begging us to leave. He wore us down. He had just begun to ride the subways by himself—during the day. We didn't let him ride at night, but he seemed so truly miserable, we decided to make an exception. We let him go home alone.

Judah didn't miss much in the second half of the concert. It was more of the same. When the house lights went up, I thanked Elena for arranging the outing and waved good-bye to my friends.

No one loves a postmortem more than Shira. She generally can't wait to analyze, evaluate, and critique after we leave an event. We even have our own name for it. We call it the "MacNeil," as in *The MacNeil/Lehrer Report,* the analytic and rather static news show that was the precursor to what is now the *PBS Newshour.* But Shira was strangely silent after we left the concert. I thought she was disappointed by the program, but when she did speak she took me by surprise.

"Ari, you told me that LSO was a bunch of old people,"

she said, clearly hurt. "Those weren't old people. Those were babes."

"Wait. Wait," I said. "That's not the whole group. Didn't I tell you about Mary and Eve? Eve's the one who looks like my Grandma Nettie."

But Shira wasn't buying any of it. "So that's who you've been hanging out with, having cocktails with on Sunday afternoons, instead of me? Finally, our kids don't need us on Sundays, and you bail? How would you feel if I found a new hobby and circle of friends?"

SHIRA

While I was going through changes as I approached sixty, Shira, eleven years younger than me, was going through her own.

Shira is one of those rare people who grow more and more striking with age. Relatives who apparently were underwhelmed when they first met her at our wedding often marvel at her beauty today. "When did she get so pretty?" they ask, as if talking about a child.

She was just twenty-two when we met, gamine-like, with chocolate brown eyes, raven black hair, an upturned nose, and the trim figure of a dancer. Shira is a raw force of nature, dark sometimes, sunny at others, smart all the time.

The first time I met her, I knew this was it. I had found her.
Or she found me.

Why was Shira uncomfortable with my LSO forays?

To understand her reaction, I had to go back to one of
our very first dates. It was evening and we were sauntering,
arm in arm, along Fifth Avenue when Shira mentioned tomatoes. "They're my favorite vegetable," I said.

"They're a fruit."

"A fruit? Are you kidding? Tomatoes are a vegetable."

A good-natured fight ensued over this matter.

For younger readers, let me pause to explain that there
was no Google in those days, no way to quickly check simple facts like the genus of a tomato. Oddly, though, I was
experienced in disputes of this kind. When I was a young
news clerk working the night shift, I'd often have to juggle
calls from semidrunk patrons at a bar asking questions like,
"Who won the 1956 World Series?" or "How many pounds
are there in a ton?" In those days if you wanted the definitive
answer—and you were tipsy—you called the *Times*.

Making a call from a pay phone—no cell phones!—to
my own newspaper for this purpose was out of the question, but there were bookstores. And some of them were
open late at night.

"Let's go to Rizzoli and look in the dictionary under
'tomato,'" I suggested.

"No," said Shira. "Rizzoli closes early. Scribner's is open."

"We're right near Rizzoli," I said. "I know it's open. Let's go."

We walked to Rizzoli. It was closed. Shira tried, without success, to suppress a triumphant smile. I let go of her arm.

We walked to Scribner's. It was open. We headed for the reference section at the back of the mezzanine and pulled out the Webster's. She was right again. A tomato is a fruit.

"Ha!" she said gleefully.

I was perplexed. Didn't her mother tell her that men don't like to feel stupid? But Shira never played the ego-boosting game with me or anyone else. She presented herself as a contender, right from the start, a force to be reckoned with.

Her will is strong, very strong, yet, over the course of our marriage, it has been my needs that have determined our family's path. My career, first as a reporter and then as a professor, dictated how—and where—we'd lived. Each of these transitions could have been fraught with tension, but in each case, Shira diffused it by making the move into an adventure—and a joint project.

That was the pattern right from the beginning of our marriage. After our wedding we set off for three weeks of overseas travel, but we cut our honeymoon short because the *Times* asked me to come back to cover the opening of the United Nation's General Assembly.

Soon after the birth of our first child, Adam, the *Times* sent me to Cambridge, Massachusetts, for a year to study religion at Harvard. Shira didn't simply "come along," she began to write freelance articles for the *Times* bureau in Boston. Years later, when we sold our suburban home and moved into university housing in Manhattan, Shira took a job as a media specialist and discovered a new, if unexpected, professional calling. A few years later when I took a sabbatical to teach and do research in Israel, Shira came along, but not until she landed a book contract to write about the experience from her perspective. When, a few years later, I spent a semester in Oxford, England, Shira expanded her business. Her new business card read SHIRA DICKER MEDIA INTERNATIONAL and listed offices in New York, Oxford, and Jerusalem. That semester, she shuttled between all three cities.

Throughout our marriage, Shira and I have had a partnership that not merely included each other but celebrated, recognized, and prized each other. But, alas, music was not something we shared. Perhaps it had to do with our age gap. When we first met, Shira was a diehard fan of the Talking Heads and also loved the Beatles, the Rolling

Stones, Squeeze, Dire Straits, and other contemporary art-
ists that made my ears hurt, with singers and groups like
David Bowie, Cyndi Lauper, Duran Duran, Supertramp,
even Madonna. She shared an apartment in Manhattan with a college friend and her Rastafarian boyfriend.
One night I picked her up and she excitedly showed me
an Elton John album—yes, an LP or long-playing vinyl
record—and popped it on her turntable. Out of the speakers came "Goodbye Yellow Brick Road," truly one of the
worst songs ever written. I quickly suggested that we go
out for the evening. "Let's go dancing!" Shira said. Surely
my idea of hell, but there was no resisting her or her sense
of adventure.

That was only the beginning of a happy, if exhausting,
courtship and marriage. In our first apartment we got ca-
ble TV, I thought, so we could watch *Masterpiece Theater*
and that wonderful but boring *MacNeil/Lehrer Report*.
But I would frequently come home to find the television
blasting MTV, with Shira singing along at the top of her
lungs and jumping on our bed.

She has a voracious musical appetite. Over the years
she's had flirtations—and lessons—with many musical
instruments, including piano, flute, and drums. She took
voice lessons and discovered a newfound love for singing

karaoke, so much so that anytime we passed a bar advertising KARAOKE TONIGHT she cast a longing glance in its direction while I tried to distract her. I joined her a few times, but decided that this was a pleasure she needed to experience with friends or by herself.

Though Shira enjoys classical music (she remembers spending a good part of her early years playing under the family's baby grand piano as her mother, an accomplished pianist, played Rachmaninoff), she is primarily a rocker girl. When she hears music, Shira moves, either on the dance floor or on the treadmill. It was one thing when I shared the cello with Judah, but when I went off on my own to LSO, something unnerved her.

It wasn't the "babes" at LSO. It was my obsession with my cello. I was putting it first. I was missing family events on Sunday afternoons and I was giving up the opportunity to be with Shira. Mr. J had called his gamba his mistress. Duke Ellington famously declared, "Music is my mistress, and she plays second to no one."

Is that what it takes to succeed? To put your music before everything? Is that what it takes to be a *real* musician?

I realized that my music needed to better coexist with my marriage. I had to make room for Shira in my musical life.

PART FIVE

OLD AND NEW

> Music remains above you: you are just striving
> to reach it. The better you become at it, the music
> moves higher, so it becomes unreachable.
>
> —GREGOR PIATIGORSKY

My middle-aged musical obsession came at a transitional time not only in my married life but in my professional life. Here I was spending more and more time on this old instrument made of wood and wire, while journalism was going wireless and paperless. The journalism that I fell in love with as a young man—the newsroom of manual typewriters and rotary phones and chain-smoking, hard-drinking newsmen—was no more. I was hired as a copy boy at the *Times* in 1973 just as computers were being introduced to a newsroom that was still very much rooted in the old world. Automobile-size rolls of newsprint were hauled into the basement each morning, and each night the presses rumbled as they printed the newspaper the old fashioned way: on paper. Outside, newspaper handlers took the papers off the presses and loaded them onto dozens and dozens of trucks that delivered fresh copies of the *New York Times* around New York—and around the country.

All of that was eventually rendered obsolete by technology that made it possible to beam images of the paper from the roof of the building at Forty-third Street to printing centers around the country and around the world. Not far behind that technology was the introduction of the Internet. Now you didn't need a paper to know what was going on; all you needed was a computer terminal and, even later, just a cell phone.

American newspapers were at first intoxicated by the opportunity to capture these new online readers. They set up websites and poured their content for free into the webisphere, convinced that this would draw new readers to their traditional product and expand their advertising base. It didn't quite happen that way. In big cities and small cities, readers abandoned the print editions and read the news online at no cost. And, much to the publishers' chagrin, advertisers were not willing to support this new venture. They had found a million other ways to connect to readers on the Web.

There was a time when newspapers had a near monopoly on reaching the public. If you were a department store and were having a sale on shoes, you put an ad in the paper. If you were an airline and wanted to fill seats, you put in a print ad with the destinations and prices. If you were looking for a job you looked in the help-wanted pages. Same if you were looking to buy a house or a car or a litter of kittens. Same if you wanted to sell these and virtually any other items. With the Web, this was all gone.

The change had enormous implications for journalism. Newspapers closed. Staffs were trimmed. Washington bureaus and foreign offices that many newspapers maintained for decades were shuttered. No one wanted to wait for tomorrow's newspaper anymore. Armed with laptops and cell phones, people wanted information—and they wanted it now. And they wanted it for free.

Journalism schools like mine had to retool. They needed new equipment, new personnel, and new strategies to attract students and convince them that they would eventually find jobs. I am not a technology person. I got into journalism because I love to tell a story. Give me a pen and a pad and I am happy. I got into journalism because it enables me to meet new people and write about them. I got into journalism because I love the thrill of a deadline and the satisfaction of meeting it.

As technology exploded around me, I staked out a position at the School of Journalism as the traditionalist. I figured there were enough people who knew HTML and Flash and Web design and Twitter. I was going to continue teaching what I was convinced were the eternal verities of journalism: good writing, interviewing, storytelling, fairness, teamwork, integrity, ethics. Someone had to remind people of these, even as we rushed headlong into what was being called "new media." And who better to do this than someone raised and reared in the old media, someone approaching sixty?

I was inspired by the words of the great conservative commentator and writer William F. Buckley, Jr., whose political philosophy I did not always agree with but who was unsurpassed in capturing ideas in words. In 1955, when Buckley started the *National Review,* he wrote that it "stands athwart history, yelling Stop, at a time when no one is inclined to do so, or to have much patience with those who so urge it."

I was determined to be the voice yelling, "Stop!" or at least, "Slow down!" as the digital onslaught arrived in America's journalism schools. I did this while some of my older teaching colleagues were setting up their Twitter and Facebook accounts.

As my birthday approached, I was teaching a class at Columbia that I had taught more than a dozen times before. It was called "Reporting and Writing 1" and it was the foundation course for everything at the school. I ran the class like a newsroom, with me as the editor in chief. The students were my staff and I instructed them on everything from interviewing and writing to news judgment and ethics. Each week, I would send them out around the city to cover news events and write feature stories. And I insisted that they stay current with news developments—and not only on the Internet. I asked them to buy a physical copy of the *New York Times,* something few in their generation did, and bring it to class on the days we met. I would use the paper to illustrate major topics in the news and trends in journalism, all the while ignoring the major trend, namely, that paper is dead.

This was a small class, with no more than sixteen students, and mine was one of numerous RW1 sections offered. In this particular year, I had six students who were designated as "new media concentrators." In addition to the lessons they had from me about the basics, they spent many, many hours supplying websites with video and audio reports. The gold standard that year was something called audio slideshows—a product akin to a talking photo album—that were proliferating like mad on news sites. Clearly these were the skills students needed to succeed.

I loved teaching RW1. I had taken the same course nearly forty years earlier and it had a major impact on how I practiced my craft. Now, as the teacher, I wanted the same for these young people. Many of our students came from excellent undergraduate colleges and some had worked for a year or two in a variety of jobs. Most of them were bright and all of them were educable. Like most good teachers, I demanded their full attention and insisted that they come to class on time.

Week after week, my six "new media concentrators" were late to class. They would enter each time with the same excuse: "We had a new media class." After three weeks of this, I erupted: "Fuck new media," I shouted. "You did not come to this school to learn new media. You came to learn the traditions and standards of journalism. New media will soon become old media. What you need to learn is journalism!"

A few weeks later, *New York Magazine* ran an article on a so-called battle being played out at Columbia Journalism over technology. The headline was COLUMBIA

J-SCHOOL'S EXISTENTIAL CRISIS. And you don't have to guess what side I was on. "'Fuck new media,' the coordinator of the RWL program, Ari Goldman, said to his RW1 students on their first day of class, according to one student. Goldman, a former *Times* reporter and sixteen-year veteran RW1 professor, described new-media training as 'playing with toys,' according to another student, and characterized the digital movement as 'an experimentation in gadgetry.'"

Aside from factual errors—I did not say it on the first day of class and I don't use words like *gadgetry*—I did say "Fuck new media," and there was no living it down. The Web is an echo chamber and my comment was picked up by magazines, newspaper websites, and dozens of blogs. There were over seventy comments alone on the *New York Magazine* website, most of them condemning me and asking how Columbia University could continue to employ such an irrelevant professor. I was called a "dinosaur," a Luddite, and worse. The embrace of the digital future was so complete that anyone who treasured the past was the enemy.

There was only one thing for me to do: I turned off my computer, went home, and played my cello.

BAR MITZVAH

There are many elements that go into a bar mitzvah, the coming of age ceremony for Jewish boys as they turn thirteen. There are the essentials, like synagogue and food, and there are the singular themes that reflect the interests of the bar mitzvah boy. We knew Judah would play cello at his bar mitzvah; it is just a big part of who he is.

The challenge was how best to find a time for Judah to play. Judah was going to have his bar mitzvah on a weekend in June at our synagogue, an Orthodox shul in Manhattan. The bad news was that the Orthodox do not allow instruments to be played on the Sabbath. The good news was that since it was the summer, the Sabbath does not arrive until late in the evening. We asked our guests to arrive for a six-thirty cello recital followed by candle lighting to usher in the Sabbath at eight. Judah prepared five classical works for the occasion, among them short pieces by Beethoven, Lully, and Dvořák. When the guests arrived, Judah took the stage and played with confidence and a sense of ownership. For four of the pieces he was accompanied on keyboard by our friend Jay, a mathematician and Wall Street analyst, who is a musician at heart. Judah's fifth piece, a solo, was an excerpt from one of Bach's famous cello suites. He felt at home with the music, the shul, and his family.

We thought it would be nice to round out Judah's concert with some additional cello playing. Judah's teacher Laura was a fine performer but she had moved to New Haven to complete her master's in music at Yale. Mr. J was sadly gone. I decided instead to invite a cellist named Noah who I had heard at another West Side synagogue, Congregation B'nai Jeshurun, where instruments are played on the Sabbath. I asked Noah if he could think of something appropriate to play for a bar mitzvah. I wasn't sure there was anything appropriate; the most famous Jewish piece for cello is Max Bruch's "Kol Nidre," based on the somber atonement themes of Yom Kippur, hardly a bar mitzvah–friendly piece. Noah assured me that there was a lot of Jewish music for the cello. In fact, many composers used the cello to express Jewish themes because they were often trying to replicate the voice of the cantor. Among the possibilities he mentioned were two pieces by Ernest Bloch—"Schelomo" and "From Jewish Life."

Noah came up with something even better. He composed a special "Musical Tribute to Judah" that included melodies from the Torah and Haftorah readings as well as songs from the Sabbath liturgy. Noah's playing was inspired and helped transition our party from a concert to the Sabbath. Noah would soon help me with my own playing, too.

As the Sabbath arrived, we locked Judah's cello and Jay's keyboard in the synagogue office and returned to the Orthodox way of keeping the holy day. We prayed that night and the next morning and Judah was called to the Torah to read and officially become a Jewish man. There was a lot of singing and chanting but there were no instruments. The synagogue was packed to overflowing with the shul regulars plus our friends and relatives. Someone on the street asked me if it was a special Jewish holiday. "For my family, it is," I responded.

JUDAH'S BAR MITZVAH CAME forty-six years after mine. Mine was marked not by the cello but by my voice. The theme of my bar mitzvah was not Bach or Mozart but the Jewish singer and songwriter Rabbi Shlomo Carlebach. Even as a boy I was deeply moved by the music of Carlebach, a German refugee who revolutionized Jewish music in the decades after the Holocaust. Shlomo, as I knew him, emigrated from Berlin as a teenager with his parents on the eve of the Second World War. While the understandable reaction to the Nazi horrors was mourning and sadness, Shlomo picked up a guitar and gave American Jews songs of hope, joy, and redemption. He produced some wonderful early LPs, which I listened to again and again in my youth. There were songs like "Od Yishama" ("May It Be Heard"), which became a standard at Jewish weddings, and "Am Yisrael Chai," ("The People of Israel Live"), which was sung at rallies in support of Soviet Jewry and the young State of Israel. These were catchy anthem-like songs that were easy to learn. But Shlomo also wrote several intricate and majestic cantorial pieces. And I sang one of them, "Mimkomcha," at my bar mitzvah. Soon after my bar mitzvah, which was held in Queens, my mother, my brothers, and I moved to the Upper West Side of Manhattan. It was there that I finally got to meet my idol, whose father, Naftali Carlebach, was the rabbi of a synagogue just a few blocks from our apartment.

The older Rabbi Carlebach looked and acted like a proper European Torah scholar. He had a formal, distinguished manner about him and a wispy white beard that seemed to hang around his face like a cloud. By comparison, Shlomo was a rebel. He was warm and physical with all those he met. He favored vests over his white shirt but rarely wore a jacket. In California's Bay Area he established The House of Love and Prayer, something of a hippie shul. He once quipped, "If I called it Temple Israel, no one would come."

I met Shlomo on his frequent trips to New York and, as a teenager, I became his part-time "roadie," accompanying him to concerts, carrying his guitar, and trying to keep him moving toward the stage when he'd stop to hug and greet fans. For me as a teenager in the 1960s, Shlomo gave me a chance to grow my hair long and rebel without ever leaving the bosom of my traditional community. I was singing protest songs but they were from the liturgy of the synagogue and I was marching for causes like Soviet Jewry and Zionism that were part of my legacy.

I lost touch with Shlomo for many years, but his music and his spirit of Jewish activism deeply influenced me. Toward the end of his life, I had an opportunity to travel to Morocco with him and a group of American doctors who had arranged a tour "in the footsteps" of Judaism's most famous doctor of the Middle Ages: Maimonides. The doctors engaged Shlomo to travel with us as a teacher and singer.

A master storyteller, Shlomo performed for the small Jewish communities of Fez and Casablanca as well as for our Muslim hosts. He was also featured at a banquet organized by the Moroccan Ministry of Culture. There he sang Hebrew songs with a twelve-piece Arab string and percussion band. It was a remarkable and hopeful moment.

I sat with him on the flight back from Casablanca to New York. He was exhausted and weak from the journey. In a moment of candor, he told me that he was not afraid of death. "When I die, I will go to heaven and there I will meet many wonderful people. I will meet my mother and my father. And I will meet Johann Sebastian Bach."

"And what will you say to Bach?" I asked.

"Well, first I will finally find out if we are related. Bach and Carlebach. How could we not be?

"Then, I will tell him, 'Mr. Bach, you wrote many wonderful symphonies and concertos, but I, Reb Shlomo Carlebach, wrote something great, too. I wrote "Mimkomcha." ' "

"Mimkomcha" starts very low, down by the cello's low C string, but then it settles for a sweet and soft lyrical section in the comfortable middle range of the male voice. The song suddenly becomes strident as the prayer gets louder and louder and asks of God: "When, oh when, will you rule again over Zion?" And then it climbs inexorably higher as it demands: "May our eyes see your kingdom, as is said in the songs of your splendor, written by David your righteous anointed one: 'The Lord shall reign forever.' "

The last notes are confrontational yet so hopeful. The prayer holds God to a standard and yet embodies a faith that God will deliver his people. By using the full range of the human voice, Shlomo is expressing a vast range of human emotion. For me, the song was never just about Zion. It was about making demands of life, of fighting for what we need, even when it seems beyond our reach.

I told Shlomo that, given the musical range and intensity of "Mimkomcha," it was the perfect song for the cello. "Yes, the cello," he said with a smile. "It was a favorite instrument of Bach—and of Carlebach, too! How I love the cello. It must be the instrument that they play in heaven."

PRACTICING

After Judah's bar mitzvah, I asked Noah to help prepare me for my birthday concert. We met sporadically at his studio on the West Side. After a year of lessons, I thought I was making progress, but Noah wasn't convinced. That's when he said that I had to practice harder and more often. Or he'd drop me. It was so out of character. I was shocked. Noah—tall and thin with his dark wavy hair pushed back high on his forehead—was a gentle soul. He had scented candles and pictures of yogis in his music studio. He made you take off your shoes before entering. It was like a shrine. Didn't I already demonstrate my commitment by coming for lessons every week?

I promised him that I wouldn't come back for the next lesson unless I practiced every day.

Practicing music is a strange art. You just don't pick up your instrument and play a song. You have to begin by playing scales, like the most basic C scale.

When he was ninety-one, Casals was approached by a student who asked, "Maestro, why do you continue to practice?" Casals replied, "Because I am making progress."

In my own way, I, too, am making progress. But it's still strange. Casals's daily routine would be the equivalent of Stephen King or John Grisham or Toni Morrison beginning each day by writing: ABCDEFGHIJKLMO NOPQRSTUVWXYZ.

But that's not all. Then the great writer would have to type: "The quick brown fox jumps over the lazy dog," that old typewriter formula that tests every letter of the alphabet. That's roughly what musicians play after they run through the scales. They do exercises just to make sure every note is clear. Then, and only then, do they take on an actual piece of music. And they play it again and again and again. After Casals played the C scale, I am told, he played Bach's cello suites. Every day. It would be like Philip Roth rereading *Hamlet*. Each day.

Somehow reading builds on itself so that what you did yesterday is still retained. When it comes to music, though, it is almost as if we are learning and relearning our art daily.

Of course, we carry our earlier lessons with us, but we bring them back each day and build on them, step by tiny step. And the longer we are away from it, even a day or two, the harder it is to recapture. Imagine being away for twenty-five years. That is why I was frustrating myself and my teachers. I needed to keep a steady momentum going to be sure I retained what I could and kept advancing.

Luckily, I had a geographical advantage. I enjoy the great luxury of working one block from my Manhattan apartment. If I had a free hour during the day, I went home and played cello. I no longer swam or jogged. I made music instead. Consistent practice—of scales, of technique, and of music—was good for my instrument, but not good for the waistline. I gained twenty pounds. I went from a thirty-five-inch waist to a thirty-eight. I had never been so heavy. I didn't like what I was turning into but I reasoned that the trade-off was worthwhile. I could always lose the weight, but this felt like my last best shot at becoming proficient in making the music that I loved the most.

THE VIEW FROM THE AUDIENCE

In addition to my regular teaching responsibilities, I occasionally do educational consulting for colleges and universities to help them develop new programs. I had been in touch for several years with Hadassah Academic College in Israel, a vocational college in Jerusalem that was interested in starting a journalism program. While most universities in the region cater to either Palestinian Arabs or Israeli Jews, Hadassah has managed to attract both. It takes advantage of its location right on the border between East and West Jerusalem and has classes for everyone from ultra-Orthodox women in wigs called *sheitels* to Arab women in head coverings called *hijabs*.

A few months before my birthday, I was granted a Fulbright scholarship to spend a month in Israel helping Hadassah. Shira and the kids were fully supportive, but I worried about my cello. Practicing was especially crucial and I did not want to fall behind. Taking my own cello was not practical; professional cellists will actually buy a seat for their instrument, but Hadassah was not about to pay for that. Storing a cello in baggage hold is a risky proposition. I've heard horror stories of splintered wood, collapsed bridges, and busted strings.

Through a musician friend in Israel, I managed to find an instrument rental business in Jerusalem and reserved a cello for the month. Before I had a chance to pick it up, I took a day trip to the city of Petra, in the south of Jordan, to see this ancient city, truly one of the wonders of the world. Petra was cut out of the desert rock more than two thousand years ago by a people known as the Nabataeans. It has been remarkably preserved and was not even known to the Western world until its discovery in 1812, although it gained real fame in 1989 when it was the setting for the adventure movie *Indiana Jones and the Last Crusade* starring Harrison Ford and Sean Connery.

I had my Petra adventure, but I paid for it afterward. The long bus rides to and from Jordan and the arduous walk along the rocky ancient city took a toll on my back. I could hardly move the next morning. I finally rolled out of bed and went crashing to the floor, then made my way on all fours to the bathroom. A friend brought me some pain medication but it provided only temporary relief. A fellow back sufferer in Jerusalem directed me to her osteopath, who manipulated the bones and muscles of my back but that relief, too, was temporary. Not only did I not get to practice cello, I barely got to the college. Most of the trip was spent struggling with my bad back. My biggest fear was flying home. I was not looking forward to sitting in a tiny seat in a cramped airplane for eleven hours. I loaded up on painkillers and boarded the flight. I made it home with the realization that I was going to have to put my cello dreams on hold.

In New York, my physician sent me to a physiatrist who prescribed a course of physical therapy. I went twice a week and gradually began to feel better. Soon I was able to sit at my desk, but the idea of wrapping my body around a cello seemed still far off. I am sure physical aliments happen to younger players, too, but they are especially threatening to late starters like me. We are more vulnerable to back pain—and every other pain, it seems—and we heal more slowly.

While this was going on, Elena sent around a note informing us that LSO had lost its performance space. The old coat factory turned actors' studio booted us out. Elena found a rehearsal space in midtown near Times Square but needed something bigger for the "open rehearsals" that LSO offered four times a year. Big spaces in New York come with big price tags, something that LSO could not afford. I called my synagogue and made a "match." LSO could play at Ramath Orah on those four Sundays at a nominal fee. To save money for a custodian, I agreed to open and close the building.

The marriage of the shul and the orchestra was a good one. On more than one occasion the orchestra was tuning up while the afternoon prayer service was getting underway. One Sunday afternoon they were short the full complement of men—ten are needed for prayer in an Orthodox congregation—and the rabbi came down to the social hall to enlist me. "Are there any other Jews here we can recruit?" he asked. Dan, the violinist, seemed pleased to accommodate. He couldn't recite the Hebrew prayers but was certainly comfortable with the choreography of the synagogue—the getting up and the getting down and the subtle bow that punctuates the Aleynu prayer.

The next time LSO gathered at the synagogue, Dan even brought his own yarmulke and asked me several times if he was needed for a minyan. His enthusiasm reminded me of what Elena had said about how people who stretch to accommodate music in their lives might keep stretching for other new experiences.

Because of my back problems I was unable to play at

our concert, but I was eager to participate as part of the audience. There were about thirty players that day and some forty guests in the hall. I took my seat among the guests, glad that I could sit without pain.

Magda raised her baton and I heard the music, imperfect to be sure, but beautiful nonetheless. But, there, from my new perspective, I noticed something that I did not see when I played with LSO. And that was the look on every musician's face. The violinists, the violists, the double bassists, the cellists—they all looked happy. They were concentrating on the music, some with furrowed brows and clenched jaw, but there were also small, almost imperceptible grins. And when Magda conducted the final notes, and held her hands up as the last sound softly faded, those grins broke out into huge smiles. Then she swept her hands upward and everyone stood. The audience continued to applaud and the musicians, beaming, seemed almost surprised by the adulation. Each person stood just a little bit taller than when the concert started.

The joy in making music was palpable. Sitting in the audience made me eager to be back on stage. I longed to wrap my arms around my cello again and resume my cello dreams.

BACK IN THE SADDLE

My physical therapist said I was not ready. My wife said I was not ready. Everyone warned me of a relapse. "You're better off if you wait a few more weeks," said Toni, the therapist, applying pressure to my lower back as I did modified sit-ups under her supervision. Toni, barely over five feet tall, was standing on a stepping stool to reach my back as I lay on the padded exam table. I struggled to lift off the table as she pushed down on my lower vertebrae. It seemed like she was trying to snap them back into place. "We are just getting your back into shape. Sitting in front of a cello is not going to be good for you right now."

"Listen to her," Shira urged when she picked me up to drive me home from therapy that day. "You're not ready. Your back is going to go out again." I reminded Shira of my birthday plans. My goal was to play in public and, damnit, I needed to practice. "You can't stop me," I said defiantly and more than a little childishly.

My argument lost some of its persuasiveness when Shira pulled the car up to the apartment. I was able to open the door but couldn't lift myself out of the car. Shira came around to help me. "Listen to Toni. You're not ready."

I did, however, have images of Mr. J playing his cello well

into his eighties, even as arthritis took its toll on his body. *The pain passes,* Mr. J explained as he played, *but the beauty remains.* And, in fact, the music was as gorgeous as ever.

I wasn't going to let some back pain stop me. Later that day, as Shira was working in the dining room, I closed the door to our bedroom and called Noah. "I'm ready," I told him. We made a date. I could easily keep Toni in the dark about this plan; Shira was the greater challenge. After all, she was working at home just feet from where I keep my cello. One day, I waited for her to go out for an appointment and, with my heart pounding, I spirited the cello out of the house and into my office a block away. Later that day, I brought my cello to Noah's studio. While I usually walk—it's about a mile away—I decided instead to take the bus. I didn't want to put more stress on my back. Plus I was already worried that Shira would somehow see me or that I'd meet a friend on the street who would later tell Shira, "Oh. Hi. I just saw Ari and his cello walking down Broadway. I thought he had a bad back?"

I boarded the bus and the driver, a rather garrulous type, greeted me loudly. "Hey, Elvis," he said, mistaking my cello for a guitar. He then leaned back in his seat and began to play air guitar. "Ba-ba-ba-ba-baaaa," he sang and laughed good-naturedly. Smiling uncomfortably, I moved to the back of the bus trying to be as inconspicuous as any six-foot-tall person bearing a cello might be. But he wasn't finished with me. "Wow. That is a big guitar! What kind of guitar is that?"

I quietly tried to explain that it was a cello. "A cello? Aren't those things heavy? Should you be lugging that around? A guitar would be easier. Or may be a ukulele. We can have a luau right here on the bus!"

I looked around at the other passengers. Everyone seemed to be enjoying his banter.

The one who would have enjoyed it most was Shira. I often think that Shira has magical powers; in fact, sometimes I think she is a witch. A good witch, of course, but a witch nonetheless. Having now spent almost thirty years with someone who has eerie psychic powers of perception, I wouldn't put anything past her. I had to wonder: Was the bus driver's behavior somehow Shira's doing? Was she in cahoots with the bus driver? And, if so, how did she know about my sneaking out with the cello?

I soon realized that no clairvoyance was involved here. It was just a New York City bus driver with a *big* personality. "God bless you!" he sang out when someone sneezed. "How was the shopping expedition?" he asked one woman with a lot of shopping bags. "Make way for the twins!" he exclaimed when a large pregnant woman boarded. I took a seat in the back of the bus and marveled at the exuberant mood he was able to create.

The driver was so busy with everyone else, I figured he'd forgotten about me. When he called out, "Ninety-sixth Street. Change here for the Number 1 train and for the M96 crosstown bus. Free transfer!" I quietly crept to the exit. But then he caught sight of me in the rearview mirror. "Bye, Elvis!" he shouted.

MUSIC CAMP BRITISH STYLE

I was on the road to recovery. I could actually sit in a chair with my cello again without feeling pain in my back and my arms. That was a big step. My playing, on the other hand, sounded much like it did before: competent at moments, but inconsistent. I felt that I had endured the pain Mr. J promised, but I had not yet found the beauty. I was no more ready for my birthday performance than for the Tour de France. I needed to do something drastic—and fast. I remembered how the ELLSO summer program worked wonders for Elena and Andrea, the LSO founders, so I thought it might just be the thing I needed to move me up the musical ladder.

How to present this to Shira, though? She had recently balked at my spending Sunday afternoons drinking with my LSO friends after rehearsals. And, as she noted at the RTO concert, not all of them were wizened old grandmothers. The only way to pull this off, I figured, was to present it as a joint venture. ELLSO, I learned, also offered arts classes at its summer program. There would be painting, fine arts, dance, and movement and Shira would be welcome to participate. As it turned out, it wasn't a tough sell at all. Shira loved the idea. In the back of my mind, I was hoping that, after a week at ELLSO, she would have to admit that classical music was the superior art form.

We were headed to Yorkshire, in the north of England, so we flew to Manchester and spent a weekend there before continuing to the summer retreat. Manchester, which has the reputation of being the gritty industrial capital of England, has been transformed in recent decades into a clean and vibrant cultural center. The city was in the midst of a huge jazz festival—with mostly amateur groups—at a half dozen outdoor locations throughout the city. We took in the sights of the city, its museums, cathedrals, and libraries, while sampling some extraordinary jazz, most of it in outdoor venues and almost all of it free of charge. We'd stop, have a beer, listen to music, and then be on our way to the next stop. On Saturday night, we managed to score tickets to a concert of opera favorites at the city's new concert venue, Bridgewater Hall. While the soloists were professionals, the orchestra and the hundred-member chorus were there for the love of it. Amateurs all.

On Sunday morning we made our way by British Rail to Doncaster, an economically depressed town in Yorkshire that was surrounded by green fields, modest country cottages, and farmhouses. The ELLSO summer program was held on the outskirts of town, on a rustic college campus complete with a golf course, sheep, pigs, and a view of wheat fields that seemed to go on forever. Perhaps best of all (from my perspective) was that, with the students gone and the Wi-Fi shut off, we couldn't connect to the Internet without going into town.

Shira, who had brought along work, initially wasn't happy but soon she also felt liberated by our cyber isolation. She relaxed. As for me, I could at last concentrate on my music without interruption. Shira and I took advantage of the relatively swanky accommodations in the campus guesthouse, but most of the other ELLSO participants stayed in the dorms, with toilets down the hall and shared kitchen facilities. Still others brought sleeping bags and camped out on the college grounds.

The people who came were not wealthy and not especially talented. What they were was devoted. ELLSO offered them something rarely found: a complete escape from life, a chance to let go of the world and dive full force into music. Music camps of this intensity are generally reserved for children or for professionals.

While I expected proper classical music—essentially eighteenth- and nineteenth-century fare—ELLSO takes pride in being musically democratic, modern, and diverse. In addition to the classical repertoire, there was jazz, contemporary music, and a wide-ranging category lumped under the title of "Gypsy, Balkan, and Klezmer Music." Many who played Bach and Beethoven during the day gathered around a campfire at night and experimented with music of quite a different sort. Shira signed up for classes in art, performance, and dance.

Most of the participants were British, but the program also drew amateur musicians from Finland, Ireland, and Belgium. Shira and I were among a small handful of Americans who came for the week of music. The participants ranged in age from thirty to almost ninety. And everyone had a story.

AARON

One of the first people to catch my eye at our very first ELLSO orchestra rehearsal was a cellist named Aaron, who was seventy-one and a retired nuclear engineer from Dorset. Aaron stood out because he played cello backward, that is, he bowed with his left hand and fingered with his right.

You sometimes see left-handed guitarists do something similar. And there are some famous lefty guitarists and electric bass players, like Paul McCartney, Jimi Hendrix, and Kurt Cobain. They are easy to spot because their guitars point in one direction while everyone else's point the other way. Guitarists who play like this usually reverse the strings so that the low strings are on the top and the high on the bottom.

Left-handed violinists, cellists, and double bassists, though, have to adjust to the right-handed way—or find another instrument. The reason is simple. While rock musicians can stand helter-skelter with their instruments pointing every which way, classical musicians must have more discipline. They sit primly on stage, grouped by instruments. Imagine a right-handed violinist trying to share a stand with a left- handed violinist. There'd be more collisions than music. Not only must they face the same way, their bows must rise and fall together. There are even notations in the music that indicate "bow direction." Being in an orchestra has some of the elements of being in the army. *We march in lockstep,* Mr. J would say. Uniformity is prized. Being part of an orchestra means playing by the rules.

But Aaron marched to his own percussionist. Not only did he reverse hands but he kept the right-handed stringing. How did this come about? "Years ago my daughter was taking cello lessons," Aaron told me over lunch one day. "I just had to try it. I couldn't very well reverse the strings—she was playing after all—but I also couldn't adjust to playing it the right-handed way. So I just switched my hands."

That was almost twenty-five years ago. Aaron picked up the cello again three years ago—in the way he knew best—with the bow in his left hand. "This is really the superior way to play," Aaron said with a smile as he demonstrated with his cello. "This way the A string is more accessible. Why reach for it all the time?" He spoke with such enthusiasm that it was almost as if he made a discovery that Pablo Casals should have figured out.

Aaron acknowledges that his playing is unconventional. "My teachers have had to adjust," he said.

"And what about your daughter, who got you started?" I asked Aaron.

"No, she stopped playing years ago, but I came back to it. . . . That is what retirement is for."

Aaron plays in an amateur orchestra in Dorset that he described as a "rehearsal orchestra."

"All we do is rehearse," he explained. "We never play in public, never have concerts. No performances. We just play for the pleasure of it."

GERALDINE

We took our meals at ELLSO at the college cafeteria and then ate, family style, at long tables. I work at a university and I know how bad college food can be, but this food set new records for inedibility. (Eventually we had to take a cab to town, find a grocery store, and stock up on provisions of our own.) The compensations for the poor food in the cafeteria were the good conversations at the dining tables. One day over lunch we met Geraldine, who was seventy years old and had a warm smile and a lilting Irish brogue. Like Aaron, Geraldine came to music through her daughter.

Geraldine was one of three double bass players—all of

them women—who came to the ELLSO summer program. If I sometimes worry about carrying an instrument that takes up twice my normal footprint, imagine what it must be like to carry a double bass. A standard double bass is six feet tall, weighs forty pounds, and is so difficult to manage it is usually carted about on a single rubber wheel.

With an instrument that size, Geraldine really had no choice but to drive and ferry from Ireland. She took up the double bass six years ago after she retired from her work as a physical therapist in Dublin. "It seemed that all my waking hours were devoted to work and family," she told me. "I'd finished supporting my children and then my eye settled over on the double bass in one corner gathering dust." It had been decades since her daughter had played.

Geraldine found herself a teacher, practiced like a demon, and eventually caught on. "I couldn't believe it," she said, "because I had never done music before." The double bass is big, but she didn't find it intimidating.

"Hey, kids can do this," she said. "It's not rocket science. I knew I could learn." Before long, she found a spot as a double bassist in the Greystones Orchestra, an amateur group in Dublin. "Was it hard to get in?" I asked.

"There was only one double bass player at the time," she said drolly. "They were delighted to have me."

I thought about all the lugging around she had to do and wondered if it kept her in shape.

"Put it this way," she said. "I have to keep fit in order to play the double bass."

Towing it around is such a big part of Geraldine's life these days that she even bought a car to accommodate it. "Last time I shopped for a new car, I brought the double bass along to the showroom to be sure it would fit," she said. Not simply in the trunk, of course. Her car is a hatchback and that is where the bass enters the car. She pushes it clear across the rear seats at an angle and it extends to the front passenger seat, which is folded down.

The trip from Ireland—in her spacious Renault Leguna Hatch—took seven hours: three hours on a ferry from Holyhead in Wales and then four hours across Britain to Doncaster. During orchestra rehearsal most of Geraldine was all but hidden behind her double bass in the back of the room, but I could make out her face. And she was always smiling.

ED, COLIN, AND CHRIS

After a long day of playing at ELLSO, many of the musicians would retire to the bar that was set up in the far corner of the campus dining room where we gathered for meals. During the day there was very little time to socialize. Participants went from session to practice room to session to practice room. Most of the daytime conversation was about a piece of music or an instrument that needed some quick repair. But in the evening, people drank, relaxed, and caught up on each other's lives. Their instruments were never far away and no one ever locked them up at ELLSO; they were strewn about the halls and along the dining room walls. Sometimes, a spontaneous jam session would break out at the bar. A musician would whip out a fiddle, another a double bass, and someone else would sit down at the piano. A woman would get up and start dancing in place and then another and yet another would join her. Soon people would be doing reels and jigs as more and more dancers and musicians joined the fray.

It was at the bar one night that I met Colin, Ed, and Chris.

Colin was old, Ed was young, and Chris somewhere in between. One night, Colin, dressed in a frayed tweed jacket and tie, stood in a corner of the room and played his violin diligently as everyone around him chatted. Tall and thin, with a music stand in front of him, Colin played the basic repertoire of a young Suzuki musician: easy classical pieces in first position. It was an odd scene since there were practice rooms open on the campus from seven in the morning to midnight. "Why here?" I asked him. "Why play in a crowded bar when you can have your very own private room?"

"Just about everybody here is better than me," Colin explained between songs. "I have to get over the fear of playing in front of people. And this helps." Colin played his songs over and over again above the din of the bar. When he was finished he packed up his violin and folded his stand. With that, the bar patrons erupted in applause. Colin took a shy bow.

Ed and I shared a beer at the bar. Ed was thirty-three, unmarried, and worked for a human rights organization in London and Geneva. He took up the violin just six months before coming to summer school and had no idea what he was in for. Like everyone else who participated, Ed was asked to fill out forms in advance about his level of musical abilities so the organizers could place him in the appropriate musical classes. Ed boldly inflated both his musical knowledge and ability. "I figured that by the time the summer came along I would know what I was doing," he said. "But to tell you the truth before I came here I never played a flat."

Ed was placed in the top orchestra group and matched for chamber music with the most proficient chamber players, but once his lack of experience and know-how were noted, he was downgraded. "Was that embarrassing?" I asked.

"No," he said with a shrug. "Everyone here is very forgiving."

A woman named Chris overheard our conversation and told how she, too, had underestimated how hard it would be to learn an instrument.

When she grew up in England in the 1960s, Chris recalled, a child had to make a choice between athletics and music. "If you were good at sports, you didn't get an instrument," she said. And she excelled in sports. She played hockey and football, joined the track team, skated, and danced. She was happy with her choices but carried a memory from her high school graduation. One of her classmates played an old English folk song, "The English Country Garden," on her treble recorder. "It sounded so beautiful," Chris recalled as if graduation had been held earlier that day. "I wondered: why wasn't I given a chance to learn an instrument?"

She continued to play sports and be physically active through a career in the British Army until a back injury sidelined her. "I was really depressed for a year and then I remembered the girl playing 'The English Country Garden.'"

In her mind, the treble recorder was too complicated. She thought the violin would be easier. "It was only four strings so I figured: how hard could it be?" In the thirteen years since she picked up the violin, she's found out. But she's never looked back. Like me, she first played with a youth ensemble and then graduated to an amateur orchestra. Her musical group has one of the best names I've ever heard. It's called the Cobweb Orchestra because so many of its musicians have retrieved their instruments from attics and dusted them off for the first time in years.

"And what about 'The English Country Garden'?" I asked Chris.

"It took me five years, but I think I finally nailed it," she said. On the violin.

People like Colin, Ed, and Chris made me feel as though I belonged.

THE MAESTROS AND ME

Unlike Ed, I *had* played a flat before. And unlike Colin, I did my practicing in one of the soundproof practice rooms. I spent a good hour a day practicing, which was not nearly enough, but then I had a very tight schedule.

The day began at 7:30 a.m. with something called "low-impact yoga for musicians" taught by a short and compact double bassist named Victor, one of the gypsy-music instructors. Here was definitely something Shira would enjoy, so the two of us arrived early, unrolled our yoga mats, and assumed the lotus position in front of Victor.

"Playing music here is like binge drinking," Victor began. "How long do you normally practice a day?" he asked us. "Twenty minutes? Thirty minutes? Well, here you are playing for eight hours a day. It is a shock to the system! You have to be prepared."

Victor, who looked like he'd been up all night—and probably was, playing gypsy music around the campfire—showed us some quick exercises that cellists can do, as he put it, "while the conductor is yelling at the violinists." The exercises involved a lot of neck rolling and pivoting in one's chair and slapping one's back. "This is like an internal massage," he said. Afterward, Victor demonstrated "relaxation techniques," including lying on the floor on a yoga mat supported by pillows and bolsters. Victor promptly fell asleep. We waited awhile for him to wake, but then realized that he was catching up on his sleep. Shira and I quietly wandered off to breakfast.

After eating, we were divided up into technique sections. Shira took off to a special program for anyone interested in painting. I was assigned to a cello section with a perfectly coiffed, smartly dressed, precise, and very proper British woman named Susannah. She could not have been more different than my rumpled and disorganized Mr. J. *Your strings are tuned in perfect fifths,* he'd say when he'd lose something or arrive late. *I'm not.*

A perfect fifth is the relationship between the four strings on the cello. The term means a tone that is five degrees above or below a given tone. And he taught me how to recognize one. *Count,* he'd instruct. *Do, re, mi, fa, so, la, ti, do. The do and the so are a perfect fifth apart!*

That is why if you can get your A string in tune, you can tune all the others. Just use your perfect fifths.

Most teachers will tune your A and leave the rest to you. But the precise Susannah wouldn't settle for that. Susannah insisted on listening to each of the four strings on each of our cellos and made the necessary adjustments. With ten people in the class that meant a considerable amount of time, but it made everyone feel special—and in tune. Susannah then went through some basic exercises that every cellist with even a modicum of training knows: playing scales, holding the bow, stretching for what are called the extended positions. Still, Susannah gave me some new ways to think about playing. At one point she compared the moment when a cellist changes bow direction to "water lapping on the shore," and at another point to "the artist's paint brush, going back and forth, back and forth." She spoke about holding the bow "with stability and flexibility," noting that the proper position of the thumb and first finger were key. "Don't grip the bow," she counseled. "Let it flow through your fingers, supported by the strings."

About three times the first hour, Susannah mentioned that her hands were small (for a cellist) and that she had to compensate in certain ways. This inspired one of my classmates, a man in his sixties named Jeremy, to recall a conversation between the great pianist Artur Schnabel and an admirer. "Mr. Schnabel," the admirer said. "Your hands are so small. How do you play piano with such small hands?" To which Schnabel is said to have replied: "Madame, I don't play with my hands."

A great musician plays with heart and mind and soul.

In stark contrast to the well-appointed Susannah was

the free-spirited Deirdre, who later in the day was in charge of my cello ensemble. To be fair, Deirdre was suffering from a head cold, but she seemed sort of spacey. Maybe she, too, had been up all night with Victor and the gypsy musicians. Her long blond hair was unkempt and she wore an oversized Indian print shirt over a pair of torn blue jeans. She was our hippie teacher, both in style and in spirit.

Deidre gave us a mighty A from her cello and sat back and listened to us tune. "Tuning is the beginning of playing. Listen to that sound! Wonderful! Wonderful!" All the A's taken together did make quite a good sound. Deirdre assembled us in a circle, saying that we needed to listen to each other. Ensemble playing in this context meant music written for four cello parts. Since we were a group of eight, two cellists played each part. We warmed up with a piece by Haydn and then tried some Bach. We did our best—and sometimes got lost—but Deirdre was a forgiving coach. She minimized our mistakes and luxuriated in our successes. "Now hold that chord. Hold it. Hold it. Hold it. Perfection!"

After an hour, I again packed up my cello, folded my music stand, and found the room for the workshop on gypsy, Balkan, and klezmer music. At breakfast, when I last saw Shira, I urged her to come and sit in on this class. If part of my agenda was to involve her in classical music, this seemed like my best shot.

Shira arrived a few minutes late and sat in the back of the room near the piano. I set up my stand and cello in the front with a group of cellists. I gave her a wave and a smile to show that I was happy she came. Suddenly, a tall and rubber-limbed man—his name was Pietr, we would learn—came bounding into the room with his violin. There was no talk of tuning our instruments and, it turned out, no need for our music stands. "No sheet music now. No music," Pietr said in a Polish accent, waving his bow at us. "You'll get the music later."

"For now, just listen. I am going to play by the air. You play, too, by the air." Occasionally he would call out a series of notes: "G, C sharp, A," he would shout. "It's the gypsy rumba."

"Play. Play. Play," he said as he leapt around the room, and we did our best to follow. "Play. There are no wrong notes." It was all by ear—or by "air," as he put it—and soon we were making music. There was a set of bongo drums in the corner and he told one of the violinists to put down her violin and start banging. He started tapping on his violin with his bow and encouraged others. Shira was dancing in place.

"My wife plays piano," I shouted to Pietr over the din. "Can she join?" Pietr nodded yes, and soon Shira was banging out chords, I was plucking notes, Pietr was carrying the melody, and a dozen other musicians were trying to keep up.

This went on for most of the hour until Pietr took one final leap, coming down as he bowed on his violin and we all laughed in amazement. He never did hand out any sheet music.

My wonder only increased when I saw that Shira had attracted a small group of musicians, including Victor, the yoga teacher, who brought his bass over to the piano when she started to play. Victor invited her to stay and jam with the next gypsy, Balkan, and klezmer session.

No one invited me. I looked at my schedule and saw that orchestra was next. Compared to the gypsy session, orchestra was a drag. It was back to the classics. The conductor was nice but colorless. I can't even remember his name. And the music was rather unmemorable—Carl Nielsen, I think. Unlike the other groups, which were made up of eight to twenty musicians, we were an orchestra of one hundred. Everyone seemed uptight. I sat next to a diminutive older woman named Linda. We seemed evenly matched. Both of us were timid players, waiting for cues from the other cellists about stopping and starting.

The conductor spent a lot of time yelling at the violinists. I recalled the exercises that Victor taught us for moments like this. When the conductor stopped yelling at the violinists, he yelled at the cellists. Finally the rehearsal came to an end. When it was over I said to Linda: "Nice meeting you. See you tomorrow."

"Oh," she said. "I hope you don't mind but tomorrow I am going to share a stand with my friend."

Had I been alone, I might have been depressed by the rejection. I was not at the top of my game. Even Linda could see that. But Shira was there to cheer me on. When I found her, she tried to assure me that Linda's motives were more social than musical.

While I seemed to be alienating people, Shira was drawing a loyal fan base. It wasn't only the gypsy musicians who wanted her. At the very first session of her dance class, she suggested some choreography and then taught it to everyone while the dance teacher looked on. She quickly took an active role in the fine arts class even though she's never painted in her life. If she wasn't exactly a witch, I figured, she was certainly bewitching.

That night at the bar, as Colin played his lonely solos and others caught up on the day's activities, I introduced Shira to my new friend Aaron, the one who plays cello backward. Aaron expressed surprise when I made the introduction. "Your wife!" he said. I was waiting for him to say, "That is your wife? I thought it was your daughter." I get that a lot. But Aaron was surprised for another reason. "My wife wouldn't come along with me!" To which I responded with a wry smile: "My wife wouldn't let me come without her."

MUSIC CAMP AMERICAN STYLE

There was, however, a music camp experience that Shira was ready to forgo. That was my next stop on the summer music circuit. After coming back from ELLSO, I decided to sign up for a program in Maine called SummerKeys. I had heard about SummerKeys from my LSO friends one afternoon at the Chinese restaurant after rehearsal. Several people were comparing camps that they had attended. A cellist named Patty said that SummerKeys was the one for serious players who had a specific musical goal in mind. No dorms or bars or communal meals there. "SummerKeys is like a musical monastery," Patty said. "It's in this remote part of Maine where there are absolutely no distractions. There is just one reason to go to SummerKeys: music."

"Will you come?" I asked Shira. Even for my adventur-ous wife, this was too much. Or too little.

"You go," she said. "I'm staying home."

SummerKeys is in the little fishing village of Lubec, Maine, the easternmost town in the United States, right at the border with Canada. One of the chief attractions is West Quoddy Gifts, which dubs itself the "Eastern-most Gift Shop in the U.S." It's so close to Canada, in fact, that you can walk over the Franklin Delano Roose-velt Memorial Bridge and have dinner in New Brunswick. Which is a good thing since there aren't any restaurants in Lubec. Or at least none worth mentioning. The local population—and local economy—have been on a down-slide for decades. The canneries and smokehouses that once gave life to the harbor area are all shuttered now, the victims of changing tastes, overfishing, and business that has moved abroad.

SummerKeys was founded by a man named Bruce Potterton, a New York City piano teacher, who bought a house in Lubec in 1991 for what he recalled was "the price of a used car." A year later he opened a summer mu-sic retreat with three pianos and fifty students. Since then, he's expanded the range of instruments to include violin, cello, mandolin, guitar, and woodwinds. The original three pianos have grown to thirteen and they are housed in churches and homes around Lubec, including two in a garage that has been dubbed "Car-negie Hall." Most participants come for a week, although some for two or three. The program draws about 250 students over the eleven-week season.

Students stay at local bed-and-breakfasts and take meals on their own. Adding to the isolation, many cell-phone networks do not reach Lubec (mine didn't) and there is no Wi-Fi outside of the Lubec Memorial Library, which was open only four hours a day, four days a week when I was there.

Lubec is a good ten-hour drive from Manhattan and three hours from the biggest nearby city, Bangor. I'm not a big fan of long-distance driving so I booked myself a New York-to-Bangor flight and looked into a bus service for the last stretch into Lubec. My decision to fly solved one problem (that long solo drive) but created another—getting my cello to Lubec.

When I told the registrar at SummerKeys of my travel issues, she said she'd be on the lookout for a cello that I could rent while there. She came through a few days later with the perfect solution. "There's a cellist from the Bangor Symphony who is coming to Lubec and she's got an extra cello she's willing to rent," the registrar said. "And not only that, but she's driving from Bangor and will pick you up from the airport."

The cellist's name was Ruth and she was just as she described herself to me in an e-mail: "Fifty-three, tall, thin, long hair and sharp nose." And a big, warm smile. She was waiting for me at the gate in Bangor and we made our way to her car, a 1996 Subaru hatchback with two cellos inside. Ruth explained that I'd be renting the cello she'd been playing since she was twelve. It was an old, slightly beaten-up Italian model with a rich sound. "I used it for my audition to the Bangor Symphony," she said. After joining, though, she bought herself a new cello, a pristine, handcrafted one from China.

As we drove, Ruth, an engineer by training, told me that she spent her career as an officer in the air force, mostly serving in bases out west. She moved to Maine in her retirement to be near her elderly parents. "I thought I'd be spending my retirement making and selling crafts and jewelry," she told me, "but then I saw this small ad in the newspaper from the Bangor Symphony. They were looking for a cellist!"

Ruth was an unlikely candidate. Her life in the air force meant a lot of moves to different places—California,

Colorado, Arizona. She always took her cello with her. She played when she could find the time but had not had formal lessons since she was twenty. After seeing the ad for the Bangor Symphony opportunity, she practiced like crazy for the audition. She was admitted as a "sub," which meant that she was technically an extra cellist but in reality played almost every concert.

Even as a sub on the orchestra roster, Ruth was suddenly in demand. After all, she could now say that she was a cellist with the Bangor Symphony. She has been called on to perform at weddings, at retirement homes, and in library concerts. She also picked up a number of young students.

"You're a professional," I observed. "Why are you going to SummerKeys?"

"There's an opening for a regular chair in the Bangor Symphony," Ruth explained. "And I want it."

Ruth felt that she had gone as far as she could working alone. She wanted a coach to help her prepare her audition piece, the Saint-Saëns cello concerto. I was only a little embarrassed when I told her what I was working on: a Bach minuet from the third Suzuki book, a piece my son Judah had perfected when he was ten. So here we were: Ruth a professional and me a late starter on our way to the same summer music camp. Any program that could teach both of us, I figured, had to be pretty versatile. I wondered if Ruth and I would, in fact, be studying with the same teacher. As it turned out, we were. The cello contingent for our week at SummerKeys was quite small: there were only five of us. The week we were there, right after the Fourth of July holiday, was a quiet one at SummerKeys. The five cellists, plus six pianists, and eight mandolin players. Not your dream week for chamber music. As it turned out, each group really kept to itself.

The cello teacher was a highly accomplished—and rather excitable—soloist and music educator named Joanne. She often brought her preteen daughter and their little dog to sessions.

It takes two hands to play a cello, the left hand to hold and finger the instrument and the right hand to bow. If there are left teachers and right teachers, then Joanne was, by far, a right teacher. All she talked about was the bow. "The bow is your voice," she told us at the first meeting of our little group. Holding the bow is an art, she said. "Hold the bow like you are holding a live bird—firmly enough so it doesn't fly off yet not so hard as to crush it."

Of course it wasn't all bow all the time, but it would always begin with the bow. "The bow is your lungs," she said a day later, "the strings are your vocal cords, the body of the cello your diaphragm." Joanne did exercises with us; one of them resembled the butterfly stroke you'd see someone doing in the pool. "Hold your arms open wide, lean back, and then lean forward and embrace your cello. Open your arms. Close your arms. Open. Close. Open. Close."

She demonstrated how we could vary the sound by placing the bow at different intervals between the end of the fingerboard and the bridge that holds up the strings. Think of it, she said, not just as variations in sounds but as different colors. Red was fortissimo (really loud). Orange, forte (loud). Yellow, mezzo forte (medium). Blue, piano. Light blue, pianissimo (quiet).

She was quite a colorful character herself, given to passionate outbursts of joy or pain at our playing. She barely sat still, at times hopping around the room to make a point about rhythm or sound.

Joanne handed us our schedules, which gave each of us time alone with her, time as a group with her, and then time—endless time—alone. We were each assigned a practice space: a walled-off room in a church or house or office to practice on our own. It made my time at ELLSO feel like a bacchanal. There were so many activities, both music and social, at ELLSO that I barely had an hour a day by myself. At SummerKeys, I practiced three and a half hours the first day and five the second day. There was nothing else to do. I kept up that level of commitment throughout the week.

Joanne made my day at our first private lesson. "You are not a beginner," she said. "You know the notes. You have a good ear. But you need to learn to make sounds with confidence." On day two she was harder on me. "You are not applying the bowing lessons I showed you. Did you practice?"

I was afraid to tell her how many hours I did practice.

She said that I needed to relax between the notes and the bowings. She dramatically pulled a hair out of her auburn head and waved it in front of me. "You must stop, but just for a hairsbreadth."

"Every note has integrity," she said at another point. She played a note and as she played she explained: "A note is born. A note lives a full life. A note dies. Now be sure to give it a chance for a proper funeral!"

Energetic was her middle name. When I had problems with my rhythm, she jumped around the room, almost as if she was on an invisible pogo stick, to demonstrate the proper rhythm.

On day three, though, her mood turned dark. "Brutal private lesson with Joanne," I wrote in my diary. "The room is cold and damp. Joanne is wrapped in a coat and is congested. Her ugly little dog is sniffing about in the corner. Joanne has lost all patience with me. She hurled the most painful insult: 'You are playing like you did before,' she declared.

"I feel like I am disappointing yet another teacher," I wrote. "I am not sure I can ever get better." But Joanne was determined. As I was playing, she grabbed my right elbow and began directing my bow, back and forth, back and forth. First she guided me firmly, then roughly, pushing my arm like it was a child on swing.

She laughed, but I could feel her frustration, even her aggression.

"I guess you've worked with all kinds of students," I said to break the tension.

She took her hand off my arm. "Little ones, big ones, professionals, semiprofessionals, superprofessionals, and everything in between."

I had to wonder: Was I the worst student she ever had?

I came away from that session dispirited. That night I sat in the chilly summer night air on the steps of the Lubec

Memorial Library, which had mercifully left its wireless connection on and sent an e-mail to Shira. "What am I doing here?" I wrote. "This was a dumb idea."

THE WEEK AT SUMMERKEYS built to a crescendo with musical performances on the last night. This was finally the time we would be able to hear the other groups—the pianists and the mandolin players—perform. And they would hear us cellists. Our little cello ensemble had been preparing a variety of pieces for the performance, mainly transcriptions by Mendelssohn and Vivaldi, since there is really so little music written for five cellos.

Most of us were anxious. We planned to play four pieces together and then each take a solo turn. Ruth, who had been working all week with Joanne on the Saint-Saëns, was in good shape, but a student named Tobie was having a meltdown over her little slice of Vivaldi. "I've got major performance anxiety," Tobie told me. But at least she had the courage to play in public. I felt so dispirited by my week at SummerKeys, I told everyone that I would not perform my Bach solo. I practiced it a hundred times but felt I was not ready for prime time, even if prime time meant a concert in the local church.

"I'm just not ready," I told Joanne at our last lesson.

I was bracing for an argument from her but she seemed relieved by my decision and didn't press me further.

The concert was a success. I played with the ensemble and then sat out the solos. I was not sure anyone even noticed.

So here I was, ten weeks before my sixtieth birthday—with years of lessons behind me, a hundred nights of practice with Judah and on my own, and weeks spent at cello camps—and still no closer to my goal. If I couldn't play in Lubec how could I play in Manhattan? I began to think that I would never get there.

The trip to Maine wasn't a total waste. I did fall in love… with Ruth's cello. I had rented it from her for a week and now couldn't part with it. I figured that even if I ended up quitting in frustration, I knew that Judah would enjoy this instrument. It did have a beautiful tone. We had been renting a half-size cello for Judah in New York. Here was the full-size cello that he could step up to when he was ready.

I FLEW HOME FROM Maine, and Ruth's cello came via UPS a few days later. Ruth sent it in a huge cardboard refrigerator box surrounded on all sides by foam rubber. It arrived in good shape—and still in tune. Although I was expecting that it would be a while before Judah was ready for this cello, he took to it immediately. It was the next step both in size and in sound. He brought out the best in the instrument. Soon after I returned to New York, we attended Judah's middle school graduation, which included a musical presentation with Judah on cello.

On stage, waiting his turn, Judah appeared supremely at home. A group of his classmates was singing, and Judah was just jamming along naturally, like you or I would hum along. At times he spun his cello around on the end pin, just like a wild jazz musician might do. It made me nervous— I had just spent thirty-five hundred dollars on that instrument—but when Judah started to play I calmed down. I listened and realized that Judah on the cello was everything I was not: strong, precise, passionate, and consistent. I watched him not in jealousy but in awe. *This is perfect,* I told myself. *Why do I need anything more? I have a son who is a cellist. And his music brings me great joy. Maybe this is the end of the story. This is the end of my cello dream. And it is fulfilled.*

PART SIX

THE BEAUTY OF AN OPEN STRING

What we play is life.
—LOUIS ARMSTRONG

I didn't even want to touch my own cello, Bill, the battered one Mr. J sold me thirty-three years earlier. Late one night, I got out of bed, took Bill out of its case, and looked at it in disgust. "You've done nothing but frustrate me all these years," I said angrily. "I hate you. I can never play you. I'm no cellist. I'm no musician. Who was I kidding?"

And, then, the cello answered me. Or maybe it was Mr. J.

Open strings.

What about open strings? I asked.

Play open strings.

Open strings, the simple act of running one's bow across each string to get the four unadorned notes of the cello, A, D, G, C—each one a perfect fifth from the one before and after it—is arguably the easiest note progression one can play on a cello. Or the hardest. Sort of like breathing. You can inhale or exhale without a thought or you can be totally mindful of every breath.

Play open strings.

Play now? In the middle of the night? I'll wake up the whole house. I'll wake up the whole building.

Just play open strings. And, I promise you, for now, only you and I will hear it.

I grabbed Bill, sat down, and began to play. Open strings.

Now remember. On each string there is a spot, a sweet spot, where you draw the most sound. Find it. Find it and stay with it. Now close your eyes. And bow.

I played open strings. A, D, G, C. A, D, G, C. A, D, G, C.

Again. Again. Again. Again.

That's beautiful. You have to think of open strings not as a series of notes, but as a song, as music. You are playing beautiful music.

I spent the better part of an hour finding the right spot, the sweet spot, and playing open strings.

Okay, Ari, enough for now. Go to sleep. But I want you to play open strings again tomorrow. And the next day. And the next. Nothing else.

And what do I play at my party? I asked. *Open strings? Maybe. But we don't have to worry about that now.*

I played open strings every day. But not only when I had the cello in my arms. I played open strings in my mind when I took the subway. I played open strings when I shopped for groceries. I played open strings when I walked the dogs. I played open strings when I taught my classes the next day. Open Strings, I was learning, was a state of mind, a continuous line of music that allowed for a serenity and calmness. Like water lapping at the shore. Like the paintbrush in the hands of an artist. Even if my hands were in my pockets, I could feel the bow moving across the string and hear its sonorous melody.

A few afternoons later, I was home playing open strings when I heard Mr. J again.

Now try the Bach.

I began to put my sheet music on my music stand.

No sheet music. Just play.

"The Bach" was Minuet no. 3, the piece that I failed to play at the concert at SummerKeys. I hadn't even tried to play it since. It's a simple melody and comes in two parts, one major and one minor. I played the first part from memory, and it never sounded better. I got lost in the minor part, but Mr. J didn't seem concerned.

*Ask Judah to help you. He'll play along and you won't
get lost.*

I hadn't planned on asking Judah. The point was that
I was going to play myself and prove to everyone, most
of all myself, that I was a musician. But playing with him
seemed right to me. Musicians play with musicians. Judah
would lift my game.

Okay, I said, *that's one song. What else?*

What else would you like to do?

I reached for the sheet music but Mr. J again stopped me.

What else can you do without music?

Come on, Mr. J, I can barely do something with *music.
How about "Mimkomcha"?*

It was the song that I sang at my bar mitzvah. The song
that the composer Shlomo Carlebach was going to tell
Bach about in heaven.

I bet I can do that, I said.

*One more thing. You told Bill you hated him. That was
good. Very good. In order to play cello, you must be able to say
"I hate you" or "I love you" with complete honesty. Once you
care that deeply, you can play "Mimkomcha" and anything
else you desire. You've learned that music is more than notes
and rhythms and strings. Music is emotion.*

Now play, Ari. You don't need Judah. And you don't need me.

I told Mr. J that I loved him. And, suddenly, I felt that he had gone away, forever. And I was alone with my cello.

HAPPY BIRTHDAY

A friend of ours who works in publishing offered us a reception room high above Manhattan for my party. It was an open, airy, and flexible space and there were some decisions that had to be made.

I wanted classical music in the background, but Shira thought rock was a better choice to put the crowd at ease. I wanted the lights on bright so I could see people; she said dimming them would create a more festive mood. I wanted lox and bagels but she ordered Mediterranean. Though our styles often clash, I have learned to defer to her on all things partyish.

On that pleasant fall Tuesday night, September 22, nearly one hundred people gathered. The invitation promised cocktails, food, and a cello presentation called "From Bach to Carlebach." As the room filled with family and friends, I drank in the sight of my party with a large measure of relief. I am not a relaxed host and yet it was impossible to ignore the fact that people were having fun. They were eating pita, olives, hummus, and falafel balls as Elton John, the Talking Heads, and the Rolling Stones—Shira's selections—played in the background. There were people from every corner of my life—from my Uncle Norman, the chancellor of Yeshiva University, to some of the mischievous young children of friends from Rosmarins, our summer bungalow colony in the Catskills. Some of my former newspaper buddies were there, as were several university colleagues. A number of my former students showed up. Editors who've worked on my books came, as did friends from my synagogue and the Bruderhof, the Christian community in upstate New York that provided us with live-in nannies and impromptu music lessons when our children were young. Noah arrived with his cello and so did some of my pals from LSO. Our Hasidic Chabad-Lubavitch friends came, too, so the fashions ranged from black hats, long skirts, and kerchiefs to bare heads, shorts, and miniskirts.

I dressed in a tuxedo jacket and wore my favorite paisley bow tie. I topped off my ensemble with my black knit yarmulke. I don't always wear a yarmulke. I don't wear one at work or while teaching, but I do wear one at home, in synagogue, and at family and Jewish community events.

It is a statement of who I am. And this was one of those occasions to declare who I am; I don't think I took anyone by surprise.

Indeed I was barely conscious of what was on my head as I happily drifted through the party. People were eating, laughing, schmoozing, and drinking. It was wonderful to see the many parts of my life come together in one place. After a short while, Shira quieted the crowd and welcomed everyone. She made a sweet toast and then opened the floor for others to follow suit. A high point was when my daughter, Emma, took the mike. Emma proceeded to reminisce about how, when she was little, she had so many things rumbling around her mind that she often had trouble falling asleep.

"My dad would come into my room, sit on my bed, and sing me folk songs," she recalled. "He sang 'Leaving on a Jet Plane' and 'Kisses Sweeter Than Wine' and 'Long Black Veil.' But my favorite was 'Brown Eyes.' At least that is what Dad *told me* it was called. It wasn't until years later that I found out the song was called 'I Still Miss Someone.' And it was about a sweetheart with blue eyes, not brown. I have brown eyes so he changed the song for me."

Turning to me with a shy smile, Emma sang:

Though I never got over those brown eyes
I see them everywhere
My dad he would rewrite folk songs
And kiss away all my tears

Emma's voice was pure, sweet, and strong, reminding me of my long-ago lost boyhood voice. She took the song I first heard from Joan Baez and reinvented it. The years fell away. I saw myself sitting on the edge of my little girl's bed, holding her hand, offering comfort in the best way I knew how—through song. Now a beautiful young woman, my daughter was singing to me, helping me on a journey to a new phase of life. I savored the magic of the moment, realizing that what I had given her had come back to me in ways well beyond my imagining.

Then it was my turn. Looking around the room, I realized that my web of relationships was built on familial bonds, friendship, music, work, and my religious life. People knew me as a teacher, colleague, friend, and fellow congregant. Almost no one there, though, knew me as a musician. The time had come to discover if I really was one. I was not nervous. I believed in my open strings.

"Over the last sixty years," I began, "I've used words, millions of words, in books, articles, lectures, and countless conversations. But some things cannot be expressed in words alone. Words cannot express my thanks to all of you for coming tonight. Words cannot express my love for Shira, who has stood by me—and put up with me and my music—for all these years. Neither can words express what a blessing my children are. The mere thought of them fills me with joy, amazement, and pride. As my beloved cello teacher Mr. J used to say, 'When words leave off, music begins.' So tonight I want to express myself in music.

"Forty-seven years ago, at my bar mitzvah, I could sing 'Mimkomcha' by the great Rabbi Shlomo Carlebach. Like Emma, I hit all the high notes back then. I can no longer sing it—my voice isn't what is used to be—but I can play it on the cello. I can, so I will. I also want to play Minuet no. 3 by J. S. Bach, but I cannot play it alone. So I have asked my son Judah to help me on cello and our friend Jay to join us on keyboard.

"And now, ladies and gentlemen, my birthday program, 'From Bach to Carlebach.'"

Judah and I took our seats and tuned our cellos. I took a few extra moments to run through my open strings. Then we nodded to Jay at the keyboard and the Bach began. Minuet no. 3 is one of the most famous Bach pieces, and while I can't easily create it here on the page, it's a dance that you've heard a hundred times on the radio or in an old movie. It's the quintessential minuet and goes like this:

Minuet

J.S. Bach

More than a song, our performance was a musical conversation, first among Judah, Jay, and me, and then among all these friends in the room. I noticed more than a few people quietly humming along.

I played expertly through the "major" opening section but then I lost my way—as I feared I would—during the "minor" section. But Mr. J was prescient in suggesting that I enlist Judah's help. While I sat out the minor part, Judah and Jay soldiered on without me. Luckily, the piece ends on a repetition of the major so I don't think anyone noticed my momentary lapses. Not from the sound of the applause, anyway.

With the Bach properly dispatched, Judah and Jay left the stage and I was alone with my cello. I took a deep breath and played "Mimkomcha," without sheet music and entirely from memory, with all of its over-the-top beauty, longing, and emotion. Again, Mr. J was right. This one I could do alone, without him and without Judah. Here's a taste of "Mimkomcha":

Mimkomcha

Shlomo Carlebach

As I pulled the bow across the strings, I could feel the "soul" of the cello emerge and connect with my soul. For a moment I was taken back to my bar mitzvah, singing with all my heart. My mother was there; my father was there; together, if only for a moment. Mr. J was there. Rabbi Carlebach was there, too, and I even think I saw Bach hovering about after listening to us playing his minuet. I found my rhythm. I found acceptance in the faces watching me. I found a sense of wholeness and joy in the moment as family, friends, music, and memory merged. It took sixty years to get there, even longer than the forty years the Israelites wandered through the desert. But the journey was worth it. I had reached my musical promised land.

FINALE

After the party, I felt that if I never played another note on the cello again, I would die a happy man. I was a musician. Maybe that wouldn't be the first thing that the newspapers would write in my obituary (if there are still newspapers), but playing music is definitely and indisputably part of who I am.

I had reached my goal, but I couldn't stop playing, of course. Since my birthday concert, many unexpected and wonderful opportunities have come my way. In my sixty-first year, as part of a citywide summer celebration, Make Music New York, I joined LSO for a concert in Central Park. Make Music New York takes place every year on June 21—the longest day of the year—and offers one thousand free musical events in public spaces throughout the city in what *New York Magazine* once called "exuberant overkill." There are similar music-making events on June 21 in cities around the world.

LSO's assigned spot was a sun-dappled pedestrian promenade overlooking Central Park's storied Wollman Rink, the ice skating site best known as the setting for parts of the 1970 Hollywood tearjerker *Love Story*. It was a clear and crisp day. As it was the beginning of summer, there were no ice skaters going in circles to the sounds of Frank Sinatra's rendition of "New York, New York." Instead, the rink had been transformed into a very non–New York City scene: a carnival that you'd expect to see at a county fair. There was a Ferris wheel, a merry-go-round, and twirling rides designed to induce thrills and nausea. Country-and-western music blared from every speaker.

The LSO members arrived one by one on the promenade and were stricken. "How are we going to compete with that?" we wondered out loud. "Why did they put us here, next to a carnival?"

Our conductor, Magda, was undaunted. She said that we would just have to outplay the honky-tonk. And we did. We played louder and with more confidence than we do at our rented space or at our usual "open rehearsal" concert space at Ramath Orah. Magda had prepared us for outdoor playing. She had warned there would be many distractions and told us that we were to ignore them all. "There are no subtleties out here," she said. "The aim is to play louder than all the distractions. And, remember: never stop playing."

Though we had only about twenty minutes of material

in our repertoire, the event organizers had booked us for an hour-long performance. While I was initially worried about boring the curious folk who had begun to assemble, our limited playlist was not a liability since our audience was a peripatetic one. Ambling past were families on their way to the amusement park below us, softball players in their team jerseys on their way to a game, couples strolling hand in hand, dog walkers with their designer pooches, Frisbee throwers, ice cream lickers, and tourists galore. Some passersby stopped to listen for a minute or two. Others took seats on the nearby park benches or found a place on the grass. Shira, in for the long haul, spread out a blanket, opened a bottle of wine, and was soon joined by our friends Scott and Ellen, who came to hear me play (and keep her company).

When our twenty-minute program was through, we simply started all over again, as if our audience had totally changed, which, to a large extent, it had. We played some of the most popular music in the classical repertoire, like Pachelbel's canon, which has a famously monotonous cello part. The cellos repeat a simple series of whole notes ad nauseum. It is a song in which the violins do all the hard work of playing the melody and the harmony in increasing complexity. The cellos just keep the beat.

I felt sorry for our earliest audience because our first run-through of the Pachelbel was a disaster. Even we cellists, who didn't have too much to mess up, messed up. Still we got it right the second time around and were downright brilliant on the third try. We also played another popular classic, Bach's "Badiniere," a brief and lively dance tune that takes its name from the French *badiner,* to jest. It was a light and sweet musical dessert.

Soon after we began the "Badiniere," a police helicopter arrived overhead and hovered there for the rest of the hour. While the police might have been searching for an escaped convict or a missing person, I imagined that they had stopped to hear us play. The helicopter drew a lot of attention, and made a considerable amount of noise, but we followed Magda's admonition—"Never stop playing"—and kept going. When we were done, one of the violinists, a man named Lawrence, quipped that we played something never before attempted: "Bach's Badinere for Strings and Helicopter."

We played what could at best be described as "incidental music." Our audience was made up of folks with a lot of other options and distractions on a beautiful summer's day. My first outdoor performance reminded me of an experiment that the *Washington Post* did in 2007 with the

violinist Joshua Bell. The *Post* conspired with Bell to play
in an indoor arcade outside the Washington Metro during
the morning rush hour just to see what the reaction would
be. With his good looks and abundant talent, Bell is one
of the rock stars of the classical music world, commanding
the attention of audiences in music halls around the world.
But during that January morning rush hour in Washington,
more than a thousand people passed by and gave him little
notice. They also gave him little money—just over thirty-
two dollars, thrown into his open violin case. All this while
he played some of the most difficult and most beautiful
music ever written on a Stradivarius valued at $3.5 million.

Like the members of LSO, Bell acknowledged being nervous as he took his place outside the subway that
morning. "It wasn't exactly stage fright," he told Gene
Weingarten, the *Washington Post* writer, "but there were
butterflies. I was stressing a little." The strangest part, he
recalled afterward, was that when he finished, there was
no applause. He usually brings down the house. The *Post*
experiment was, of course, an effort to show that people
don't appreciate what is around them while others may
well pay too much for high culture (a ticket to a Joshua
Bell concert can easily command a hundred dollars a seat).
Weingarten's article, "Pearls before Breakfast," opened an

international discussion about our relationship to public art and music. The story won the *Post* a Pulitzer Prize for Feature Writing.

I can safely say that our ragged band of LSO amateurs received a good deal of respect, encouragement, and attention during our Central Park gig—and a lot more applause than Joshua Bell did.

MY CELLO ESCAPADES AFTER my birthday were not only classical. One night Shira and I went to a music club in SoHo to hear a performance by our friend Ricky Orbach, a guitarist and songwriter who had just come out with a CD called *New Midlife Crisis*. True to its title, Ricky was a husband and father and jeweler who was returning to music after many years away from it. His music drew from several rock 'n' roll genres. After the gig, we shared a drink with Ricky and I told him about my own musical midlife exploits. "You play the cello?" he asked. "I wrote a song, 'Shoshana,' that cries out for a cello. You must play with me."

A few weeks later, Ricky sent me a link to a recording of "Shoshana." It sure was a depressing song, with lyrics like "Shoshana says, 'My husband's gone. Yes, the car crash, three injured kids.'" Perfect for the cello, I thought.

The music was challenging. It required a great many position shifts up and down the fingerboard, but this was not an occasion to invoke the spirit of Mr. J. He'd gotten me to my sixtieth. That was enough. I decided to figure out "Shoshana" on my own. And I did.

I joined Ricky for a four-hour rehearsal at a Lower East Side studio. There was Ricky, two guitarists, and me. At one point, when Ricky's drummer showed up stoned, I felt like I was in a bad rock documentary (aka a rockumentary). At home, I practiced like crazy and couldn't wait for our date, my first rock gig, at a club on the Lower East Side called the National Underground. Shira dressed in a short black dress, thigh-high kneesocks and Dr. Martens. I wore my regular professor clothes. She looked like she belonged far more than I did. The gig was called for eleven o'clock on a Thursday night and, as I approached the club, I was excited to see the name of our band listed in white chalk on a board at the entrance.

I glided past the bouncer by taking a cool stance and pointing to the cello on my back. I went down a flight of stairs and heard the deafening sounds of a punk rock band whose name was on the chalkboard before ours. Aside from the band on stage and the barmaid, the place was pretty much empty. Soon Ricky's guitarists showed up.

(The drummer never did.) Then some of Ricky's fans. A dozen, in all, including Ricky's wife and mine. It was a big crowd compared to what the band before us drew.

We rocked. I ended up playing "Shoshana" and one other of Ricky's songs, called "Completion," which also called for a cello. Then I took my seat in the audience, ordered a drink, and celebrated my first rock 'n' roll gig.

GRAND FINALE

Judah's musical journey has also taken some unexpected turns since my sixtieth birthday. Soon after his bar mitzvah, Judah became obsessed with rock music, especially the Beatles, Bruce Springsteen, Green Day, and the Red Hot Chili Peppers. My initial reaction was to remind him of all the cool rock bands that used cellos. I tried to introduce him to the music of Apocalyptica, Rasputina, Murder by Death, Cello Fury, and Aaron Minsky, also known as Von Cello. Judah was unimpressed and, frankly, so was I. "Okay. I've got an idea," I said. "Let's get an electric pickup so we can amplify your cello. That way you can play *rock* cello."

Judah and I headed to a store in Lower Manhattan called David Gage String Instruments, a showroom and workshop where cellos and double basses were scattered across two stories of an old industrial loft. We entered the workshop area, where we saw dozens of instruments in various stages of disrepair laid out on workbenches. Luthiers walked from table to table like so many emergency room doctors. The only difference was that they were wearing worn leather smocks instead of white coats.

In addition to sales and repairs, David Gage String Instruments makes, sells, and installs a product called "The Realist," an electronic pickup device that amplifies string instruments. "That's the ticket," I said, and off Judah's cello went to the workshop to get amped. It took only minutes and then we began to shop for an amplifier to plug in the new equipment.

William, our salesman, showed us some expensive professional amps, selling for a thousand dollars and more. I told Judah that this was way beyond what we could afford. "Then why did we get the pickup?" he asked quite reasonably.

William saw my distress, looked around to be sure no one heard him, and said, "What you need is a bass guitar amp. That will work fine with your cello. We don't sell those here, but you can get one for pretty cheap at Guitar Center on Fourteenth Street."

From the moment William uttered those words— "Guitar Center on Fourteenth Street"—our lives were not to be the same. When we entered the shop for the first time, I might as well have smashed Judah's cello over the threshold. We bought the bass amp that day and Judah hooked it up to his cello that night, but *rock* cello never caught on in our house. Guitar Center did. The store became Judah's Xanadu. He was then nearing fifteen and just beginning to make his way around the city on his own. Every free afternoon, every early night off from school, Judah headed down to Fourteenth Street, ogling the electric bases and guitars like older teen boys ogle girls. Within the next twelve months, he not only acquired a bass amp, but an electric bass guitar, two six-string electric guitars, an acoustic guitar, strings, picks, guitars stands, and a portable amp.

Before my eyes, Judah was morphing from a classical cellist into a rock musician.

To the strains of *Fiddler on the Roof,* I hear Tevye pleading with his youngest daughter Chava not to marry Fyedka, the handsome young non-Jewish Russian. "Never talk about this again," he exclaims at the mere suggestion of their union.

Like Tevye, I thought I could stem the tide.

I wasn't about to let him stop cello. He could play guitar if he wanted to, I said, but cello was his first instrument. His cello teacher would continue to come each
week. And, let me make one thing perfectly clear, young
man: no guitar lessons.

Then one day Judah asked if I would come into his
room. He had long before put away the toys that he so
loved in his youth: Pajama Sam, Pokémon, Yu-Gi-Oh!
Most recently, Judah went through a Nipponophile phase,
in part fueled by the Japanese comic called Manga that he
devoured. He had taken to labeling with Japanese trans-
lation stickers everything in his room and in the house,
from his bed (*shou*) to the toaster in the kitchen (*tosuta*)
to the dogs that ran amuck in the house (*inu*).

But, now, on this night, there was little evidence of his
old obsessions. Instead there were four guitars suspended
from hooks above his bed. Wires and amps and distortion
pedals crisscrossed the floor. His cello had recently been
relegated to the living room, on an instrument stand near
mine.

"Dad," he announced, "I want to stop cello lessons."

Even though the evidence for this declaration was everywhere, I was disbelieving. "Judah, you've been playing

cello since you were six. You love the cello. You are great at it. You can't."

"I'm not going to stop playing, Dad. I just want to stop lessons. I'm too busy with school and my friends and my music."

"Okay," I said, getting desperate. "I'll make a deal with you. You continue taking cello lessons and I'll get you a guitar teacher, too. That way you'll be good at both."

"I don't need a guitar teacher. I can learn on my own. And I don't need a cello teacher either. I'm finished with lessons."

My mind went back to when Judah was a little boy and we took the subway together to Suzuki class with his very first cello teacher, Sujin, the one who put dinosaur stickers on his music workbook when he mastered a piece. If, when we set off for a lesson, Judah complained that he was tired or "not in the mood," we'd just stop at the Baskin-Robbins on the corner and order an ice cream. Within minutes, his worries would be forgotten and he'd happily go off for his lesson with Sujin. Now, there was no ice-cream cone in the world big enough to change his mind.

And there was no stopping his musical hunger. After all, Tevye can't stop Chava. She marries Fyedka anyway.

Judah taught himself to play electric bass and guitar.
And he did it by using the medium I most feared: the
Internet. Fuck new media, indeed! To learn to play his
favorite songs, he downloads "tabs," a form of musical notation that indicates fingering rather than musical pitches.
It seems like cheating to me but it works. He plays the bass
parts of songs together with his favorite bands' YouTube
videos. He sounds like he's part of the band, which is just
what he aims for.

Judah saves his birthday and holiday money for his
Guitar Center excursions and to buy hard-to-find rock
songbooks at vintage shops around New York City. He
jams before going to school (with, at my insistence, the
amp off) and when he comes home (with the amp at full
blast). And we triumphed over our downstairs neighbor
András. Fed up with us, he moved. In his place, we got a
neighbor who doesn't seem to mind the music.

Judah jams in the music room at school during classroom breaks. He plays in several bands, all of them con-
figurations of various musical friends. One of his bands,
Blue Velvet, took third place in a local battle of the bands.

To me, Judah's transformation was sudden and dramatic. One day my youngest son was a sweet-faced, sincere boy with round checks and curly hair; the next he had

slimmed down, perfected a sullen appearance, wore his hair spiky, acquired a black wardrobe, and was borrowing my electric shaver. Most unfairly of all, he started playing music with Shira, who until this point had left his musical education up to me. How was this possible? After all, it was *me* who sat through a decade's worth of Suzuki lessons with him. It was *me* who picked him up from school early every Tuesday afternoon so he could get to the Morningside Orchestra. It was *me* who took him to Suzuki camp in New England for five summers running.

Now instead of cello duets in my living room, I was coming home to find Judah, a guitar strapped to his chest, playing music with his mother. Shira was at the piano banging out "Stadium Arcadium" or "Heaven" or "Goodbye Yellow Brick Road" or another song I couldn't stand. They went over riffs and worked out harmonies endlessly. And even when they weren't at their instruments, like when we were all in the car, they sang their favorite songs, often arguing over lyrics. Back home they'd consult lyrics.com. Then they'd download the ringtone. (My favorite ringtone is "ringggg-ringggg." Who needs anything more?)

This was a betrayal of mind-boggling proportions. How did this happen? *She really is a witch,* I thought.

I grieved over the loss of the compliant cello prodigy I had been cultivating. Maybe it was just as well that the spirit of Mr. J had left me. This would have been too painful to witness. But then, again, Mr. J, like Johnny Cash, had said that all music was from God. Maybe rock, too.

I had to admit that bringing a guitar to high school was far cooler than schlepping a cello. And I did see that the cellist in my son was not lost. Clearly, Judah took everything that he learned on the cello—melody, rhythm, intonation, pitch, and performance—and applied it to his new musical interests. And he hasn't abandoned the cello. When performing at school, he will move with fluidity from guitar to cello to bass and back again. He tells me that he plans to play cello in the orchestra when he goes to college. Recently he has been teaching himself the piano and mandolin and has begun to arrange, compose, and record music. He will often lay down voice, guitar, piano, bass, and cello tracks and mix them all on GarageBand to create original music that he posts and shares on the Internet. He even has his own YouTube channel.

While I have struggled for decades to master one instrument, the cello, Judah does not see the lines between instruments that I do. He is musically fearless. He plays songs—and writes songs—that express his happiness, his sadness, and everything in between. While I set aside time for practice, he just plays. While I keep a diary, he keeps logs of his songs. They reveal as much about him as words say about me. Music is his ultimate form of expression. It connects him with the musicians he admires. It connects him with friends. It connects him with Shira.

And it still connects him with me.

JUDAH AND I KEEP our cellos on special upright instrument stands in our living room, one cello at each end of the big black leather couch. The cellos stand there within easy reach, poised for the moment when musical inspiration strikes.

One day I carefully take Judah's cello from its stand and bring it over to a chair. I position myself opposite Bill, thinking that perhaps I have the power to conjure up the spirit of Mr. J one more time and entice him to play with me. I've heard him come through Bill before.

I plant my feet squarely on the floor, place the cello between my legs, take the bow in my right hand, and gently glide it over the strings.

I play my open strings, running the bow between the bridge and the fingerboard, careful to find the sweet spot where the sound resonates most vibrantly. I look at Bill but

I do not hear a note. I do not hear a word. No one else is home. And no one else is playing. This is just me.

My playing fills the house. The sound fills the air. It is rich, full, and luxuriant. Every note is perfect. Time slows, and slows, and slows, until it stops. I lift my left hand to the strings and find third position. Without effort or intention, I am playing Rabbi Carlebach's "Mimkomcha." I feel time actually unfurling, slowly moving back, and back, and back, until I am at a place where I was before the cello, before fatherhood, before marriage, before adulthood. Suddenly, I am no longer a sixty-something-year-old man in my apartment in New York, but I am a boy singing in the synagogue, reaching for the high notes.

Effortlessly, I hit each one with grace and energy and passion. The happiness I feel is followed by a burst of inspiration that leads me to the Bach minuet that I struggled with for years. I stop to see if Bill will join me, help me through the difficult passages, but he remains silent. I am on my own.

The melody glides easily off my bow. The music flows naturally and with a fluency that Bach himself would admire. My left hand dances across the fingerboard and the music surges through the house. My music. Just me. The cello has transported me beyond time, beyond space, beyond myself. It is playing me as much as I am playing it.

Everything that Judah ever played on this cello, everything that Ruth of the Bangor Symphony played—music that I was sure was beyond my abilities—is now coming through my hands, though my bow, through this cello, through me. I am working my way from one glorious piece to another. Vivaldi, Mozart, Breval, Boccherini, Fauré, Tchaikovsky, Saint-Saëns, Beethoven. With ease, I am playing songs that I never played before. They are fully familiar to me; they are mine. The world has stopped, and it will stay that way, as long as I hold the cello in my arms. With it, I can transcend time, even transcend my own abilities, and embrace the world with all the joy, sadness, and beauty that only music can express.

ACKNOWLEDGMENTS

My greatest thanks goes to the men and women who, over the years, have taught me to play cello, in particular Heinrich Joachim, Noah Hoffeld, Laura Usiskin, and Suzanne Saba Hughes. Noah was especially helpful in putting this book together by providing valuable feedback as well as the musical notations that adorn the final chapter.

Several friends read the manuscript at various points and I would like to thank them for their guidance and input. These include Dr. Isaac Herschkopf, Carolyn Starman Hessel, Samuel G. Freedman, Jack Schwartz, and Rabbi Elie Spitz. I also got my family involved in this project, and I would like to thank my cousins Debra Kolitz and Deb Kram, and my children, Adam, Emma, and Judah. My most dedicated and helpful reader was my wife, Shira, who read through several iterations of this book and encouraged me at every turn. While I welcomed everyone's contributions, all the shortcomings of this book are mine and mine alone.

I would like to thank the members, conductors, and administrators of the various orchestras that I joined over the years for allowing me to play with them and for talking with me about what the music means to them. The best part of writing this book was doing those interviews. My thanks to the InterSchool Orchestras of New York, the Downtown Symphony, the East London Late Starters Orchestra, and the New York Late-Starters String Orchestra.

I am grateful to Eric Hanson for the enchanting drawings that grace these pages. Finally, I want to thank my editor, Amy Gash—ever-positive, patient, and inspiring—and the whole team at Algonquin.